FAMILY TIES THAT BIND

FAMILY TIES THAT BIND
A Self-Help Guide to Change through Family of Origin Therapy

Dr. Ronald W. Richardson

Self-Counsel Press
(a division of)
International Self-Counsel Press Ltd.
USA   Canada

Printed in Canada.

First edition: 1984; Reprinted: 1985

Second edition: 1987; Reprinted: 1987; 1988 (2); 1989; 1990; 1991; 1992 (2); 1993

Third edition: 1995; Reprinted: 1996; 1997; 1999; 2000; 2001; 2002; 2005; 2007 (2); 2010

Fourth edition: 2011; Reprinted 2012

Library and Archives Canada Cataloguing in Publication

Richardson, Ronald W. (Ronald Wayne), 1939–

Family ties that bind : a self-help guide to change through family of origin therapy / Ronald W. Richardson. — 4th ed.

(Self-Counsel personal self-help)
ISBN 978-1-77040-086-3

1. Families. 2. Family psychotherapy. 3. Self-esteem.
I. Title. II. Series: Self-Counsel personal self-help

HQ734.R53 2011   306.87   C2010-908109-9

Cartoons by Carole Klemm © 1995

Cover and inside images
Copyright©iStockphoto/Russian dolls family - isolated/orhancam

Self-Counsel Press
(a division of)
International Self-Counsel Press Ltd.

Bellingham, WA   North Vancouver, BC
USA   Canada

CONTENTS

NOTICE TO READERS

Laws are constantly changing. Every effort is made to keep this publication as current as possible. However, the author, the publisher, and the vendor of this book make no representations or warranties regarding the outcome or the use to which the information in this book is put and are not assuming any liability for any claims, losses, or damages arising out of the use of this book. The reader should not rely on the author or publisher of this book for any professional advice. Please be sure you have the most recent edition.

All of the case histories reported in this book are an accurate reflection of what has actually happened in the lives of my clients. However, in every case, identifying characteristics have been changed to protect confidentiality, and occasionally the histories of two or more people have been amalgamated into one for a clearer and more effective presentation of theory.

Most of the case histories are about women, which is merely a reflection of the greater number of female clients I have had. It seems that women are more often willing to seek professional help to work on issues in their lives. This is usually a sign of their greater health and motivation.

ACKNOWLEDGMENTS

In a *New Yorker* cartoon, a publisher at his desk says to a somewhat surprised author, "Well, it's good. But people just don't write books all by themselves anymore." That was certainly my experience with this book.

I learned the concepts of how families operate from the writings of Dr. Murray Bowen of Georgetown University. He is one of the earliest pioneers and practitioners of family therapy. Most of what is in this book is based on his research and work with families, which began in the early 1950s. I have simply tried to translate his concepts into popular language. I learned how to implement the concepts in my own life and in my clinical practice from Dr. David Freeman of the University of British Columbia. He has been a caring and more than competent guide in helping me sort through the meaning and usefulness of family of origin work.

But the book would never have existed without my wife, Lois. A professional editor and an author, she first suggested the idea of a book on family of origin therapy for laypeople. After I did my best at writing it, she rewrote and reorganized much of it to make it clearer and more readable, often over my protests, but finally with my gratitude. This book is as much her effort as it is mine. The chapter on sibling position is entirely her work.

And, of course, I thank my own family of origin — my mother who was an enduring example of love and support; an unknown father; aunt; uncle; cousin; grandparents; great-grandparents — all who knew me as a child and who I have tried to get to know better as an adult.

Chapter
1

INTRODUCTION

The more intensively the family has stamped its character upon the child, the more [the child] will tend to feel and see its earlier miniature world again in the bigger world of adult life.

— Carl Gustav Jung

Life in the family of origin (the family a person is born and raised in) is a tremendously powerful experience for everyone. And the impact of that experience is not restricted to childhood. The way we see ourselves, others, and the world is shaped in the setting of our family of origin. The views we develop there stay with us throughout life.

At some point, most of us leave our families of origin physically, but we rarely leave them emotionally. Even if you put an ocean between you and your family of origin, or never return home again, you will continue to re-enact the dynamics of your original family in any new family you establish. The specific content may well be different, of course.

For example, you may do many of the very things your parents did, even though you always swore you wouldn't. No doubt your parents swore the same thing about their parents, who swore the same thing about their parents, back to the first cave man and woman who swore they'd never be the apes their parents were. At times, this decision to be different can take interesting turns.

Example

Annette, a divorced parent with children aged 14, 12, and 9, complained that her parents never liked or approved of what she did. She made a rule for herself as a parent to always praise her children

1

and let them know how much she liked them. To her surprise, her oldest child told her one day, "Mom, the problem with you is you're always telling us how good we are and we can't believe you because we never hear the other side!"

One of the most difficult things in life is to gain emotional separateness from that powerful early family environment and not continually repeat it or react against it.

The purpose of this book is to help you find new ways to deal with that family environment — to have a better life here and now by learning a different way of dealing with your "leftovers" from there and then. If you can look at the unfinished business of your past in an appropriate context — the environment of your family of origin — your present and future experiences in life can be more positive. You can be more in charge of your own life, less defeated by undesirable events, and better able to create for yourself the kind of life you want.

Think about how you feel when you visit or phone your parents. Do you feel or act similarly to the way you did when you were living at home? How long can you last before the old feelings start? Five minutes? An hour? Two days? What happens to you when things start getting tense? If you can last more than three days before acting or feeling like a 13-year-old again, you probably don't need this book. Most adults, however, tend to act in ways they wish were different. Some attempt to fit in as peacefully as possible. They deny their own feelings, do what their parents want, and don't rock the boat.

Others make a point of being the opposite of what their parents want and expect. They are perpetual rebels.

Some try to show their parents how they failed as parents and work on improving them. Many just have as little to do with family as possible. They are emotionally distant and rarely visit or communicate with their families.

All of these ways of relating bear testimony to the power of our families in our lives. Most of us have not learned how to be close to these significant people while continuing to feel like our own persons. We find ourselves reacting to them, rather than doing what would make sense to us in our most objective moments. Yet, until you can be an independent adult with your family, it is unlikely you can be this way with anyone else in an intimate relationship.

The same issues end up getting dumped into new intimate relationships: marriage (legal or common-law, same-sex or opposite-sex), children, work, friendships. The extent to which a satisfying adult life can be established is dependent upon how well you learn to deal with these forces in your family of origin.

One way to do this is through family of origin work. The goal of this work is to change your experience of yourself in your family of origin and, by extension, in your present relationships.

None of us really has a choice about whether to deal with our families or not. Even choosing not to deal with them is a way of dealing with them. You can't be free of your early experiences by denying their significance or ignoring them. Your early experiences are bound to repeat in your present life with different characters and in different contexts.

Doing family of origin work is one way to begin changing this self-defeating pattern. Some people do this work with a counselor, or a family therapist, but you can also do it on your own. In fact, people were using this approach long before family therapists started taking credit for it. A natural part of becoming a mature adult is to reassess the earlier relationships with family and make adjustments in them.

Doing family of origin work requires an understanding of how families function. Chapters 2 to 7 will help you with this. Those chapters discuss specific family dynamics that you will want to examine in your own situation. Throughout these chapters are questions and exercises for you to think about and do. You don't have to sit down and write out answers to the questions, but you will benefit most if you read each one carefully and let it simmer in your mind as you read further. Do the exercises that make sense to you in your situation and that you feel comfortable with.

Understanding the concepts and being able to identify the dynamics at work in your family are only the first steps. This book is not intended to provide insight only into your family. For that insight to be meaningful, you will have to change your behavior and way of being in your family of origin. Chapter 8 gives you the instructions for doing the practical work. But don't cheat and skip straight to that chapter; it won't make a lot of sense unless you know something about the theory that comes first. Take your time and be patient. Once you have waded through all the theory, you will be amazed at how well and simply it all fits together.

Even those who have been out of touch with their families for years can do this work; old relationships can be renewed. If your parents are dead, friends or relatives can be contacted for information about your childhood environment.

People of any age can and do use this method for changing themselves, although it is easiest for those who are at least in their late twenties.

Younger people are often still trying to get away physically and can't yet handle the stickier emotional separation. However, no matter what your age, dealing with your family of origin can be difficult, and you may find it easier if you have some support. If you are fortunate enough to know a therapist who is familiar with family of origin therapy, you would do well to use his or her services. Because family of origin work requires you to do all the work, these therapists usually call themselves coaches. In fact, any good listener who can provide the support you need and ask appropriate questions can be this kind of coach. Sometimes a group of friends can provide this for each other in regular meetings set up for this purpose.

A spouse or lover does not make a good coach. Even the best of them find it extremely difficult to remain neutral about family matters. Your spouse's involvement can only complicate things for you. Your coach must be able to ask you a lot of questions to help you begin to think differently about your family. Spouses are more likely to tell you what to think despite their best intentions.

You also won't get very far with this work if you do it with someone (spouse or therapist) who believes that your parents are to blame for all your problems. You'll just end up feeling justified for your anger or hurt, or whatever your feelings are toward your family. The point is for you to change — and you must do that by looking at your family in a different light.

One warning: Some people, who are deeply troubled or come from families with severe emotional problems or a history of sexual abuse, should not attempt to do this work without professional help. However, most average people with only the normal complement of problems can do this work without involving a third party.

In any case, there are two important things to remember as you work your way through this book:

(a) Keep the emphasis on yourself. Just as no one else is able to make you change, you cannot make anyone else change. So don't even bother trying. (A nice side effect of your changes may be that other family members change in a positive way, too, but that is not your goal.)

(b) You need to be motivated. Do you really want to change the way things are in your life right now? Doing family of origin work is hard work, and it is not for everyone. It is not an easy-answer, quick-fix program. It requires a commitment of time, energy, and thought, but the rewards are great for those who hang in there.

The following story of Sue and her family shows how effective family of origin therapy can be.

Example

Sue was going home for the first time in six years. She didn't really want to make this trip, but she felt she should. Her five younger brothers and sisters had let her know how hurt Mom and Dad were that she never came to see them.

Sue had left home at the age of 19, after the last of a long series of fights with her parents that had gone on all through her adolescence. Both parents scorned her "radical" political views, but Sue saw Dad as the primary problem and was quick to point out his shortcomings as a parent. Dad demanded she give up her modern ideas and be a "woman" and knuckle under the way his wife had. He did not hesitate to use his knuckles — and fists — to keep the family in line. Sue was the only one who ever openly challenged him. She refused to be controlled.

After their last fight, Sue announced that she was leaving home. She still vividly remembered walking out the door alone, carrying her own luggage. Dad, in the living room reading the newspaper, barely looked up to say goodbye. Mother was crying in the kitchen, not daring to risk the possible confrontation that might result if she were to see her daughter off.

There had been a few cards and brief phone calls since then, but nothing else. She knew her parents would be waiting to see if she had changed. Sue realized she had done little since leaving home that her parents would approve of. She had spent three unmotivated years in college because she could think of nothing else to do. She began living with Steve, her boyfriend, while he was still an art student, and when he graduated, they traveled in Europe for a year. After returning they got married, but it was not a satisfying marriage for either of them. In fact, this trip was a way to separate for a while — they had been arguing so much. She was currently working part time at a low-paying job in a group home for teenagers hooked on drugs. Steve worked occasionally as a freelance commercial artist but most of the time he experimented with his painting.

At the dinner table when Sue arrived home, her sister asked her about her work and the conversation turned to teenagers and drugs. Mom tried unsuccessfully to change the topic. Sue shared her sister's beliefs about why teens got into trouble. She thought they were victims of uncaring, authoritarian parents, a sick school system, and a corrupt society.

After trying to control his reactions, Dad was unable to keep quiet any longer. "Damn it, you haven't changed a bit! You're still spouting your hippy-dippy, commie junk. You and your worthless husband are wasting away your lives, living off society. Aren't you ever going to grow up?"

Sue had hoped to avoid this, but she was not going to let him get away with that kind of remark. She came back at him with her best attacks from the past, honed with more "evidence" gathered over the past six years. The scene ended with Dad walking out, Mother going to the kitchen, and the others quietly disappearing. Sitting alone at the table, Sue decided to go home as soon as she could get a flight the next day.

Four years later, Sue went home again. She had changed her mind about never visiting again. In fact, she had made three short trips in the previous two years. Her feelings about going home this time were much, much different.

Shortly after that disastrous trip four years earlier, her marriage became even more difficult. She and Steve were ready to separate, but decided to seek marriage counseling first. As they discussed their marriage with the therapist, both began to see how much their conflicts related to their family backgrounds and the sensitivities developed in those earlier settings. Both were trying to resolve in their marriage the issues that remained unresolved with their separate families of origin.

The therapist had asked how much they knew about their parents as people, not just as parents, and what they knew about their parents' own family background, childhood, and parents.

The therapist encouraged them to seek the answers from family members. After some hesitation, they began to write letters and make phone calls to parents, brothers, sisters, aunts, uncles, and grandparents, asking about the family. Slowly the pieces began to fit.

In the process of doing this, Steve and Sue's relationship with each other began to change. They stopped attacking each other every time they disagreed about something. There was less blame and withdrawal. They still had conflicts, but they were able to think through positions and state them more clearly, without reacting so strongly against each other.

Each began to find more meaningful direction in work and more satisfaction in life. Both felt they were finally growing up.

Sue's experience with her family became more satisfying as well. She began to appreciate them, and feel less shame and anger. She was more receptive to seeing what they had done for her as parents. But more importantly, she began to see them more fully as people who had their own problems.

On her fourth trip home, Sue's feelings were very different from that first return trip. On the surface, things didn't look too much different: Dad didn't have much to say when he picked her up at the airport; Mom still acted as if her life was relegated to the kitchen. But Sue reacted differently. She told her dad the things about herself she wanted him to know and she no longer felt angry at her mother for being so passive. When her dad disagreed with her and called her the names that used to make her furious, she was able to stick up for her point of view without lashing out at him in uncontrollable anger. Neither of them walked out on the other; instead they "agreed to disagree." At times, she wanted to say to him, "I love you," but she didn't think either of them could handle that much closeness. At least not yet.

There is nothing magical about the changes that happened in Sue and her family. You can change your experience with your family too. Going home again can help you to finally really leave home, which means growing up emotionally. When you can be yourself in the difficult setting of your family of origin, you can be yourself anywhere, and you will be better able to deal with current relationship problems in a flexible and appropriate way.

Chapter 2

FAMILIES ARE STRANGE CREATURES

Though in one sense, our family was certainly a simple machine, as it consisted of a few wheels, yet there was this much to be said for it, that these wheels were set in motion by so many different springs, and acted one upon the other from such a variety of strange principles and impulses — that though it was a simple machine, it had the honour and advantages of a complex one — and a number of as odd movements within it, as ever were beheld in the inside of a Dutch silkmill.

— Laurence Sterne,
The Life and Opinion of Tristram Shandy, 1762

1. THE HIP BONE'S CONNECTED TO THE THIGH BONE — HOW FAMILIES WORK

A family, as Sue found out the hard way, is not just a collection of individuals who simply "do their own thing." A family is more than the sum total of the persons in it, just as the hand is more than the sum total of five fingers and a palm. Each finger on the hand develops its own "personality" in relation to the rest of the hand. If one finger is lost, the whole hand is affected and can no longer function as it has; each finger has to adjust to that loss and learn some new functions.

Families are the same way, but a lot more complicated than fingers. Each family member develops a unique personality, but not in a vacuum. Your personality developed in relation and response to the other personalities in your family. And all of their personalities developed and changed in response to yours. Every member of a family, whether it's mother in the same room or great-uncle Henry who ran away to Australia 30 years ago, affects every other family member in some way. Nothing happens in isolation in a family. If one member of a family gets sick, the other members are affected and adjust to it in some way. Then the sick member adjusts to their changes, which brings about further change. It can go on and on, like a hanging mobile being blown and shifted by the wind. Every time one part of a mobile adds or loses weight, or moves toward or away from the center of gravity, all the parts hang off balance until the changed part returns to its original place or the other parts adjust themselves.

Every time a family member gets in trouble with the law, does well academically, gets a promotion, has a baby, or is hospitalized, the rest of the family compensates. This compensation happens whether the original change is good or bad. The change itself creates the imbalance that causes other family members to scurry around trying to restore the equilibrium.

The ways individuals balance themselves or create imbalance in their family determines the general health and happiness of all the family members.

Example

As an adult, Consuela was quite close to her mother. They talked on the phone or saw each other daily. After her mother died, Consuela tried to rebalance her life by getting more involved with her 13-year-old daughter, Maria. This increased closeness with Maria affected the family in a number of ways. Consuela became even more remote from her husband, who was jealous of her relationship with Maria; Maria became more distant from her 11-year-old sister; that sister became jealous of mother and Maria's relationship. At just the point in her life when Maria would normally be shifting her allegiance from the family to her friends, she could not abandon mom. She resented her mother's dependence but felt guilty about her resentment so never expressed it — even to herself. As a result, she got upset over little things and had stomach aches that her doctor could not diagnose. He sent the family to a therapist, where the imbalances began to be discussed openly.

QUESTIONS

1. What major changes have happened in your family of origin in the last 20 years? What births, deaths, marriages, departures, or other changes in status occurred?

2. How did family members react to these changes?

3. How have you or your brothers and sisters been involved in these changes?

The balancing and counterbalancing that goes on in our families of origin affects us for our entire lives, even if we never have any contact with family members after adolescence. Next to our biological drives, it is the single most powerful influence on us. No one escapes its impact.

In Consuela's case, the death of her mother affected the whole family in ways they would not have anticipated.

Try this exercise to see how your family mobile balances itself.

YOUR FAMILY MOBILE

Either change or stop doing one thing that you normally do with or for someone you are emotionally close to. For example, if you normally kiss your wife goodbye in the morning, or call your husband at work, or ask your son each day what he did in school, don't do it for two weeks.

- What are your feelings as you think about changing this one thing? How do you feel when you actually change your behavior?

- How does the other person react? If there is no overt reaction, are there any other changes in the person? What are your reactions to the reactions?

When two people get married, we tend to think of their relationship as a separate entity. Their happiness and problems in living together seem to be purely a product of their own personalities and entirely up to them. For example, we see only Joe and Sara in this relationship, as in the diagram:

Joe   Sara

However, the reality is much different. Any marriage is merely a link-up of two mobiles. It may not look very romantic, but Joe's and Sara's relationship actually looks like this:

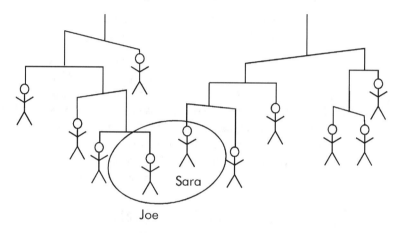

Sara

Joe

Joe and Sara became who they are as a result of their experiences in their families. They are very much affected by what went on there and by how their families dealt with the imbalances in their lives. Joe and Sara tend to see and evaluate each other primarily in terms of their own family mobiles. Their self-expectations and expectations about each other's behavior come out of their family experiences. Their marriage is more than the two of them coming together. It is two family mobiles bumping into each other.

One example of how this works shows up in their fights about money. "He is a spendthrift," Sara says. "Money burns a hole in his pocket." She wants to put more money into a savings account. "She is too tight with money and unable to enjoy it," Joe says. "What's the point of having it if you can't enjoy it?"

The attitudes they have toward money, and saving and spending it, were shaped in their own families of origin. They may be the same as or the opposite of their parents, but their attitudes developed in response to their parents' ideas about money. Sara's parents, who barely made it through the Great Depression emphasized the necessity of saving and

Sara decided they were right about it. Joe's parents told him similar things, but placed more restrictions on his spending. They called him irresponsible no matter how little he spent. Now, when Sara raises the issue of Joe's spending, it revives the battles he had with Mom and Dad. He responds to Sara just as he did to his parents. Joe sees Sara's statements about money through the filter of his own family experiences. She does the same thing.

QUESTIONS

1. What are some of the conflicts you have in your present intimate relationships that trouble you?

2. Are you able to trace any of your reactions to experiences or conflicts in your family of origin? For example, what is one upsetting feeling you have when with a friend or spouse? Who in your family of origin could evoke a similar feeling in you? What parallels are there between the two situations and the way you deal with them emotionally?

2. EAT YOUR SPINACH — RULES IN THE FAMILY

Every family, and every relationship, has rules. Rules are a set of expectations about how people should conduct themselves in various kinds of settings and circumstances. Rules say what is allowable and not allowable. They also say what the consequences are when the rules are obeyed or disobeyed.

There are two kinds of rules — spoken and unspoken. Families develop many different rules of each kind. The spoken rules are the easy ones. They include such things as: "Don't interrupt." "Say please." "Don't play loud music." Everyone in the family knows what these rules are, and they can be openly talked about, perhaps even debated and changed.

The unspoken rules are a different story. They may be understood and even agreed upon by family members, but they are not openly acknowledged or discussed. If mentioned, they may even be denied by those who are the strongest believers. For example, in some families, it is not all right to be angry, but it is acceptable to be depressed. No one would think of stating it this way, but the rule is: When things don't go your way, you cannot be angry, but you can be depressed.

In other families, fear is not allowed, or it is allowed only for the females. The rule is: When men in this family feel scared, they are supposed to deny the fear, even to themselves, and act angry instead.

Sad feelings are not allowed in some families. The rule is: Always appear happy and keep a stiff upper lip. This unspoken rule is being expressed when a crying child is told, "Look at the bright side," or "Don't be a baby."

The unspoken rules

Arguing is not allowed in some families. Family members are expected to be agreeable at all times. The rule is: If you get angry, go away until you have cooled down and come back with a smile. In other families, conflict is the only acceptable way to relate. The rule is: Arguments are better than being too cool and indifferent; you show you care by fighting it out.

QUESTIONS

1. What were some of the openly acknowledged and spoken rules in your family?

2.   What were some of the unspoken rules about having and expressing feelings?

In Joe and Sara's fights over money, their different attitudes toward spending money is only part of the problem. They each also learned different rules for dealing with conflict in their families of origin.

As it becomes clear to Sara that Joe doesn't want to save, she gets more upset and emotional. She is angry and hurt. She says, "You don't care about our future." This is upsetting for Joe who isn't used to such behavior in his family. He gets tense and attempts to calm her down by saying things like, "Let's talk about this when you're calmer." When that doesn't work, he refuses to talk to her at all and says, "You're being crazy and irrational. I'll talk to you when you make sense." Sara thinks he means that he'll talk about it when she's ready to come around to his point of view. She then gets even more upset over both what she considers his condescending style and his refusal to settle the issue with her. That's when she starts to feel like throwing things, and often does.

In Joe's family, conflicts were not argued emotionally. People had a brief confrontation and then went to their separate corners until they could come out smiling. The issue was rarely discussed again, and few clear, joint decisions were made. In Sara's family, when there was a conflict, people dealt with it then and there. After the shouting, it was over, and people were friends again. Often, a decision was made at the end of it all.

In this case, Joe and Sara have different expectations about how they should deal with conflict. The two family mobiles are crashing into each other. Joe thinks Sara is not living according to the rules. "If she loved me, she wouldn't shout at me. She'd be more considerate. Love is not getting angry and shouting."

And Sara says to herself, "If he really loved me, he'd deal with my concerns about this issue instead of ignoring me and putting me down. He'd be more considerate. Love is letting your partner know how you feel, even if you have to shout."

Both think they are loving and the other is unloving. Both think they handle conflicts correctly and the other doesn't. Both think the other is breaking the rules. They have assumed that they have the same definition of love and that the other is purposely being hateful. This simple example shows what happens when the unspoken rules are controlling behavior — no one really knows what's going on.

The basic purpose of all these rules is to control the way people in the family relate. They keep things in balance if everyone plays the game. Each person added to the family gets a lesson in the rules. Children in the family learn them in two ways. One is by experiencing their own anxiety when a rule is broken and the other is experiencing a parent's anxiety.

QUESTIONS

1. What were the spoken and unspoken rules in your family about handling differences and conflicts between family members?

2. Were there different conflict rules for different people or different sexes? Did age affect the rules?

3. Have you continued to have the same rules for conflict in your present relationships, or have you changed them? Are your present rules just the reverse of the old rules? Are they really new?

4. What are the rules for conflict in your partner's family of origin and how do they conflict with your own?

Anxiety is not a nice feeling. It is basically a fear of the unknown, which is worse than an ordinary fear of some specific thing. Anxiety leaves you feeling vulnerable and powerless. Most people, especially children, will do almost anything in order to avoid it. So we all learn to behave in a certain way to avoid feeling anxious, even if that creates other uncomfortable feelings. We will choose to feel depressed or paranoid, for example, rather than to feel anxious. The person who can make you feel anxious is in control. Parents learn this early in dealing with their children. When children break a rule (spoken or unspoken) parents may use physical punishment, but the most effective punishment is the withdrawal of love (or the threat of withdrawal). This punishment plays on the fear of abandonment that everyone has when young. The threat of abandonment usually provokes enough anxiety that a child will change in order to avoid it. A common example of this is when a father tells his two-year-old son it is time to leave the park. The child says "no" and won't move. The father could just pick up the child and cart him off, but instead uses psychological force. He walks away and says, "Okay, you stay here, I'm going." After the father gets several yards away, the boy begins to follow.

In different guises, this same threat of abandonment is used to control many aspects of a child's personality. Because young children need their parents so much, they will suppress the parts of themselves that the parents find objectionable rather than experience the anxiety. In effect, children say to themselves, "I can't make it on my own. I need my parents, so I better not do anything that will lead to losing them." This is how we learn that it's often dangerous to be ourselves.

Even if a parent doesn't use physical or psychological punishment when a child breaks a rule, the child can learn about the rule because the parent becomes anxious. Young children have to be extremely sensitive to anxiety in their parents for the sake of their own survival. Just as young children keep tabs on the physical presence of their parents, they develop an awareness of their emotional presence as well. They know, whether anyone says it or not, when a parent is upset. Frequently, children feel responsible for their parents' anxiety (of course, sometimes they are the trigger for their parents' anxiety). If a child has done something and the parent then feels uneasy, the child will feel uneasy, too. If it happens often, the child will probably stop that behavior. The child tries to be self-protective by following the rules and taking care of the parent.

QUESTIONS

1. What happened to the level of anxiety in your family when unspoken rules were broken? Who would begin to object, make an issue of the behavior, or become anxious? For example, if anger was not acceptable, what would happen if someone began to openly express anger in the family? How would it be controlled?

2. What would happen if a spoken rule was not observed?

3. What rules do you think you are still observing? How do you react when they are broken?

Chapter 3

YOU NEVER TALK TO ME — CLOSENESS AND DISTANCE AMONG FAMILY MEMBERS

In Genesis it says that it is not good ... to be alone, but sometimes it's a great relief.

— John Barrymore

1. COME CLOSER — NOT TOO CLOSE

Each of us needs closeness (togetherness) on one hand and distance (separateness) on the other. We need affiliation, support, security, love, and approval; and independence, autonomy, freedom, and self-direction.

These apparently opposite needs stay with us throughout life, changing in their intensity depending on the environment and our stage of life.

As infants, we are totally dependent and desire nothing but constant attention from parents. Around the age of two, we begin risking some separateness from our parents, but we don't want them out of sight. We get anxious if they are gone for any period of time or if we think we have no access to them. As we grow older and become more secure in our belief that our parents will be available when we really need them, we can tolerate increasingly longer periods of separation.

Eventually at adolescence, we demand separateness. We believe we are more or less capable of an independent life, but even then we continue to be dependent in many ways. This dilemma is part of the pain and confusion of adolescence. In young adulthood, we set off on our own, physically leaving the family. After a period of time, we meet someone and begin a new struggle with our needs for closeness and distance with that person.

Use the following exercise to determine how you have become closer or more distant in your relationships.

YOUR EMOTIONAL RELATIONSHIPS

Draw a diagram, using circles for females and squares for males, of your family of origin when you were ten years old. Include each family member and yourself. Place them either close or distant to each other depending on what you think the emotional relationships were at the time. Here is an example:

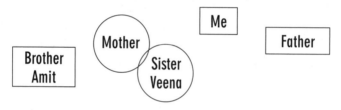

Try doing a similar diagram for when you were ages 3, 6, 14, and 18. Do you notice any change in positions over the years? What do you think was the impact of these changes?

Draw a diagram of your present relationship with your family of origin.

Now draw a diagram of your current family of spouse or partner and children, if any. If you are single, draw what you think your family would look like. Do you see any similarities in these family diagrams?

We are usually attracted to people who have the same needs for closeness or distance that we do. Of all the people who are available as potential partners, we inevitably manage to find one with a nearly identical comfort zone on the thermostat of closeness/distance. This doesn't mean, however, that we act the same or express the same needs. That would make things too easy. It usually looks as though one person wants more closeness and the other more distance. A says to B, "Talk to me more," and B says to A, "Leave me alone." But what is really going on is that each person is helping to keep the balance by playing the role of either a pursuer or a distancer. If one of them changes roles, the other usually changes, too, to keep the family mobile in balance. For example, if the pursuer starts distancing, at some point the distancer will get anxious and start pursuing.

Couples often go to a marriage counselor with exactly this problem. Most often it is the woman who complains about the coolness of her husband, while he complains about her clinging. But if she begins to be less needy and more independent, he often starts becoming more dependent on her. He might not admit his need of her, but will start saying that she is too selfish or is neglecting the kids, for example.

People in all kinds of relationships tend to be either pursuers or distancers most of the time, but everyone is capable of playing both roles. Traditionally, women have been the pursuers in emotional closeness and men have been the pursuers in sexual closeness. The pursuers have trouble being themselves without a close intimate relationship. They are people who need people and they are basically motivated by fear of abandonment.

Distancers have trouble being themselves when they are close; they tend to feel suffocated. They are the people who want to "do it my way," and they are basically motivated by fear of engulfment.

In better functioning relationships, the partners are able to be both ways in a number of situations; they can identify and express their needs for both closeness and distance.

QUESTIONS

1. Who were the pursuers in your family of origin? Who were the distancers?

2. In what situations was your mother the pursuer? The distancer? In what situations was your father the pursuer? The distancer? What about your brothers and sisters?

3. To what extent was it okay for you to be either emotionally distant or close in your family? Was it acceptable for you to alternate in your needs or was there an expectation to be only one way? If so, what did you do?

4. Who would become most anxious if you wanted closeness or distance? How did you act if someone wanted either of these from you?

5. Which role have you adopted in current intimate relationships? Does your role vary depending on who the relationship is with or depending on the issue? How does the other person react to your pursuit or your distancing?

Couples sometimes stay together and fight over the issue of closeness/distance every year of their relationship. While one continually demands more closeness and the other demands more distance, neither recognizes that they are both helping to maintain their comfort level, which was established in their separate families of origin. A couple like this may end up getting divorced and then later marry someone else, believing that the new mate is just what they really wanted and is totally different from the former mate. Invariably they again choose someone with the same comfort level. The whole drama will be replayed a second time, though perhaps with different content and perhaps with other roles. What they fight over may be different, and the former pursuer may become the distancer, but the basic pattern stays the same.

People can change their level of comfort on the closeness/distance scale. They can move up or down on it a few degrees, but they still work at finding a balance in their relationship at their new level.

2. APPEARANCES ARE DECEIVING

One of the tricky things about closeness and distance is that most outwardly independent people are only pseudo-independent. They use distance as a way of controlling their fears about closeness. They may have tremendous needs for closeness, but have become afraid of it, so they distance instead.

The person who has no apparent need for closeness will choose for a partner someone who insists on togetherness. This partner represents the other side of the person's own ambivalence about closeness and distance. The two of them will, in fact, have the same comfort level. However, the relationship will be turbulent because of their different ways of handling their needs for closeness or distance. They will fight over their emotional thermostat the way some people fight over the furnace thermostat setting. One turns it up and the other comes by and turns it down; neither is happy about the other person's actions, but they manage to keep the temperature at a fairly constant level midway between their extremes.

The paradox of this is that even those who openly admit their need for togetherness are not usually capable of intimacy. True intimacy means having an accepting, open relationship with someone who is different from us. People who need constant closeness and togetherness have trouble accepting that others are not the same as them. They have trouble thinking of themselves separately. They talk about what "we think" and how "we feel" rather than what "I" think or feel. They insist: "We think about each other before we think about ourselves." They talk about sacrificing for others and not being selfish. They espouse the values of love and compassion for others but often use those things in a manipulative way. They feel responsible for the happiness of others, and if someone is not happy ask, "What have I done wrong?" They also blame others for their own unhappiness.

Those who use distancing as a way of keeping the balance talk about lack of support, caring, or consideration from the pursuer who is nagging them. However, the favorite response of distancers is silence. They simply withdraw. They also say, "I don't know," as a way of avoiding an encounter with others.

But remember, even though they look very different, the pursuer and the distancer in a relationship have the same basic need for togetherness.

Try the following exercise to see how distancing and pursuing affect your relationships with people.

DISTANCING AND PURSUING

Decide whether you are usually a distancer or a pursuer. Then select a person who plays the opposite role in a significant relationship of yours. For a week, try playing the other person's role — the opposite of what you are usually like with that person. Try doing a better job at playing that role than the other person does. If you are playing the distancer, be even more distant than the distancer usually is. Take note of what reactions and changes, if any, occur in both you and the other person.

Now do this with a parent or another family member where you tend to have one set pattern. What happens to both of you when you change this pattern?

---

3. ALL THE WORLD WANTS A MOMMY

The need for togetherness originates, like everything else, in the family of origin. Somewhere around the ages of six to nine, we begin to realize we are not going to get all the love and acceptance and security we want from our parents. As we get older, we slowly begin to develop a fantasy, which tends to peak in later adolescence, that somewhere out there is an ideal mate who will fill the emptiness we feel. We look forward to a time when we will be "in love" and experience true togetherness. What we didn't get from our parents, we imagine we will get from our mate.

A major hidden expectation is that this person will provide for us the long-awaited bliss of perfect union. The more starry-eyed among us think this person is "everything I ever wanted in a mate." The rest of us just think we will be able to turn that person into everything we ever wanted.

Example

Judith's father had been hospitalized several times with emotional problems. Her mother was a highly anxious person and had little ability to nurture others. As the eldest of three, Judith basically ran the family and kept things going. She dreamed of the day when she would escape and live a more normal life.

After the failure of her second marriage, she sought therapy, wanting to find out what was going wrong. In spite of being an attractive and capable woman, her adult life was turning out much differently from what she wanted.

She discovered during therapy that she had been expecting her husband to give her the good feelings about herself that she never got from her parents. She had been the emotional pursuer, but since she had never really experienced closeness, she was, in fact, uncomfortable with it when it was available. She had chosen men who were basically at the same comfort level of closeness/distance as her family. They were unable to provide what she both wanted and feared. When she dated men who could give it to her, she distanced and did not continue the relationship.

The more children are deprived of nurture and guidance in early years, the stronger their fantasy later that this special person will make everything better. They fall in love with the image of what they think this mate will provide. When the reality strikes, they feel angry, frustrated, hurt, and disappointed. Then they usually try to figure out how to get what they want from the other person.

People usually find fault in someone when they're not getting what they think they need. If they blame themselves, they try to find out what the other wants and then act on that to win approval or love. They give to get.

If they decide the fault is with the other person, they try various methods of changing that person. These methods may include everything from flattery to criticism to physical attack.

Example

Lela, the oldest of three sisters, had a chaotic childhood involving many moves and times when she lived with relatives rather than her parents. Her parents fought a great deal, and Lela resolved that when she married she was going to have a stable, happy family. She developed the skills and techniques she thought would help make this happen. However, she married Hank, an emotionally remote only child, who did not share her ideas about family. He was basically a loner and did not have much interest in parenting or in family life. He just wanted someone who would look after and admire him. What they wanted from each other was in strong conflict. Each handled the conflict the way conflict had been dealt with in their family of origin. Lela began to sound more and more like the "bitchy" mother she had hated, and Hank was increasingly like his distant father who had many affairs and stayed away from home. They moved a lot and fought a lot. Jani, their 19-year-old daughter, started saying exactly what Lela had said at that age: She wanted a "stable, happy home life." Yet she behaved with her boyfriends the way her mother behaved with her father.

Both Lela and Hank had developed expectations about how their marriage should be, based primarily on their unfulfilled childhood needs. They got married thinking the other would automatically provide what they wanted; indeed, they insisted and demanded that the other provide it. They blamed each other and demanded that the other change. In fact, neither one was comfortable with closeness, and daughter Jani was the same way.

Too much togetherness can be as threatening in a relationship as too much separateness. It is not uncommon for couples to fight after they have had a particularly good and intense lovemaking experience or some other kind of intimate closeness. This happens because they fear that by becoming too close they will lose their own identity or become too vulnerable. Many people have the misconception that to be close means having to give up their individuality. That can be just as scary as having too much distance in a relationship. The challenge is to learn how to be close, open, and accepting, and still be a unique and separate individual. It can be done, as you will see.

Chapter
4

YOU'RE NOT BETTER, JUST DIFFERENT — DEALING WITH DIFFERENCES

Whom we are related to in the complex web of family ties over all the generations is unalterable by us. Obviously, family members frequently act as if this were not so — they cut each other off because of conflicts or because they claim to have "nothing in common." But when family members act as though family relationships were optional, they do so to the detriment of their own sense of identity, and of the richness of their emotional and social context.

— Elizabeth A. Carter and Monica McGoldrick,
The Family Life Cycle

1. I SAY TOMATO, YOU SAY TOMAHTO — ANXIETY ABOUT DIFFERENCES

Most people get married thinking their spouse is like them and they both want the same things in life. It doesn't take long to discover this is not the case. Most of us are lucky if we make it through the honeymoon without a major clash over differences: what time to get up in the morning, where to eat dinner, how to squeeze the toothpaste tube. This is just the beginning of potentially serious conflicts in the relationship. Both partners begin to wonder if they made the right choice; maybe they made a mistake and married Dr. Jekyll. Certainly this person isn't what he or she first appeared to be. It looks as if the two of them are not going to have the blissful togetherness they expected.

No two people can have an intense, intimate relationship without discovering significant differences between them. This is normal. It's how we deal with those differences that creates problems. Most of us see these differences as a threat to our ideal of a good relationship: continual harmony between two people who want the same things at the same time.

When differences emerge, most of us try to make our partners more like us. After all, what is an intimate relationship for but to have a like-minded companion walking side by side with us down the road of life? When we find out that it's not going to be like that, we become anxious. The normal pattern then is to think the cause of our anxiety is the behavior of the other person. Jose says to himself, "The reason I am unhappy is because of her. If she were different and acting the way I want her to, then I wouldn't feel bad. It's her fault."

"Why can't a woman be more like a man," Professor Higgins cried. And we echo him: "Why can't you be more like me?" Of course, we are usually too sophisticated to admit this is what we want, so we hide our intentions behind our thoughts. We think our spouses, children, bosses, or whoever "ought" to be a certain way. Often we say, "You should" or "You ought to," but what we really mean is "I want you to." For example, when Betta says to Stefan, "You should talk to me more," she is disguising her anxiety about their differences. What is really at stake is that she likes conversation and Stefan doesn't. If she were not anxious about the difference, Betta could say, "I would like you to talk with me." That would be an honest expression of what she wants. Or Stefan might say to Betta, "I'd like some time to be quiet," rather than, "You talk too much."

These dynamics are not restricted to marriage of course. They are present in every relationship where there are differences (which is just about every relationship) and at least one of the people grows anxious about the differences. Parents and children, friends, coworkers, ethnic groups (where differences can be more visible), labor/management, liberals/conservatives, and nations all have to live with differences.

QUESTIONS

1. What were some of the major differences in your family of origin? How did people in the family handle these differences? Did some people handle particular differences better than others?

2. What are some of the major differences between you and your partner? How do you handle differences? In what ways are you trying to get your partner to change? In what ways is your partner trying to get you to change? How do you react?

2. DO IT MY WAY OR ELSE — THE DEMAND FOR SAMENESS

As mentioned, when one person in a relationship is anxious about differences, he or she usually tries to get the other person to change. Betta tries to get Stefan to be a talker like she is and Stefan tries to get Betta to be a loner like he is. The pressure is on for more sameness. However, it's not easy to change someone else, as those who have been trying for 50 years will testify. Usually, those being asked (ordered) to change respond in one of four basic ways. They will —

(a) comply,

(b) rebel,

(c) attack, or

(d) cut off.

These four ways of reacting are discussed in detail below. You may recognize some or possibly all of these tactics as having been used in your family. You may even recognize some you have used yourself. Most of us use them all at one time or another depending on the circumstances, but we usually have a favorite.

Whether you are the changer or the changee, it is important to realize that these strategies are common ways of reacting when there is a demand for change. They do not happen in isolation. No one person is the good guy or the bad guy; we are all simply attempting to cope with our anxiety about differences and the threats to our need for closeness or distance in the family. In this discussion about these strategies, the focus tends to be on spouses, but the same things happen in other relationships, intimate or casual.

2.1 "I only want what you want, dear" — The compliant ones

The compliant ones react to a demand for sameness by pretending there really are no differences. This is seen most commonly in marriages where the couple presents a united front to the world; even their own kids don't know what they really feel. They avoid conflict because it emphasizes differences; togetherness is their ideal. These people may be more or less aware of their needs for separateness and difference but they think these needs are wrong and destructive to the relationship, so they ignore them. These couples appear to have a good marriage because they never fight. However, they often find other ways to assert themselves. The bedtime headache-to-avoid-sex cliché, is just one example of the power of a compliant wife. She is able to deny to herself and to him that there is any conflict between them, while maintaining her separateness by claiming to be, or being, ill.

Example

Amanda and Abe took their 16-year-old daughter, Polly, to a therapist saying she had become "sexually promiscuous." They denied having any problem in their marriage and said they were very happy with each other. When asked how they talk with Polly about sex and sexual feelings, they said they didn't talk with her except to give prohibitions. When asked how they talk with each other about sex, they admitted that they didn't, and that in fact they hadn't had any sexual contact for a long time. Amanda said that she had never enjoyed sex. Abe said he had gotten this message from her and refrained from pursuing her sexually or even talking about it. He complied with her wish, and the anxiety about sex in the relationship was displaced onto the daughter whose symptoms pointed to where the problem was in the marriage.

Whatever form it takes, the basic need for compliant ones is "peace at any price." They fear conflict and, especially, the separateness that this conflict would seem to indicate. It may appear that just one of the partners avoids conflict, but actually both have trouble with it and together, covertly and unconsciously, they use this approach to cope with their anxiety. Both fail to fully explore the other's beliefs, principles, thoughts, and feelings about an issue. Instead, they deny the differences and never really get to know themselves or each other very well. They remain unaware of the advantages their differences may bring to problem solving.

Remember, the compliant one is not necessarily without power. There is a great deal of power in being the apparently powerless underdog, in being the one who sacrifices self for others and says, "Don't bother about me, you go ahead and do what you want."

The underdogs have a talent for being able to create guilt in others, and they usually know how to use it well. There is usually some kind of "trade-off" for the underdog. Unconsciously the underdog thinks:

"Okay, I'll give in and go along on this and this and this, but you sure better come across later on that." If you don't come across, the underdog may risk the conflict by crying, "I did this and this and this for you and you won't even do that for me!" Even if it doesn't work this time, the underdog has added to your burden of guilt for next time.

One of the ways compliant ones deal with the lack of intimacy is to become very involved in something outside the marriage relationship. It could be in church or community activities, in an aging parent, in a hobby, or in a job. Many compliant mothers become overly involved with their children, which is usually damaging to both mother and child. Many children whose parents operate in a compliant manner with each other have difficulty later taking responsibility for themselves because the over-invested parent did everything for them. By being so involved with the children, the parents are able to avoid looking at and dealing with their own differences and needs for closeness or distance.

Compliant people are often the ones who become physically or emotionally ill. Their struggle to cope with differences might manifest itself in frequent headaches or back problems, a mild depression, alcoholism, an inability to hold a job, cancer, heart problems, or severe emotional disturbances that require institutionalization.

Example

Roberto had been an alcoholic for eight years. In his sober state, he couldn't stand up for himself in his marriage. He was compliant with his wife the way he had been with his authoritarian mother. However, all that changed when he was drunk. Then he was full of rage and said things to his family that, everyone agreed, he wouldn't say and couldn't really mean when sober. As he learned to speak up for himself in the relationship and be more assertive, his drinking decreased dramatically.

QUESTIONS

1. Who used compliance in your family of origin? In what covert ways was the compliant one powerful? What were some of the trade-offs?

2. Are there ways today that you choose to be compliant rather than openly acknowledge the differences between you and someone else?

Of course, as you have probably guessed by now, the compliant person is not only taking care of his or her anxiety by being sick. The other person has the same level of anxiety; by being sick and providing a focus for all that anxiety, the compliant one helps keep things in balance. If the sick one gets well, the couple will work out some other way to avoid facing their differences.

2.2 "I did it my way" — The rebels

Rebels look as though they want distance and independence, but because real independence is too scary, they stay close and act rebellious. When A says do this, B does that, even if doing this would have been better.

The rebel never learns how to be secure about being different. The rebel is so involved in rebelling, in not doing and not being the way others want, that the rebel never decides what he or she does want. The rebel who is busy fighting against other people's goals isn't able to set his or her own goals. For the rebel, independence means doing the opposite of what others want. However, by doing this, the rebel is still being controlled by someone else. The other person is still calling the tune; the rebel just plays the flip side.

Of course, to be a successful rebel, you need someone to rebel against. Most rebels can easily find people who are quite willing to play the heavy and tell the rebel what to do. And that person, the authority, is always right: "Do that and you'll — be sorry; get hurt; not pass; be fired; have an accident." When the prophesied doom happens, the authority can say, "I told you so. You should listen to me (be like me)." But then that person jumps in and picks up the pieces, and takes on the responsibility of whatever disaster befell the rebel. So the rebel seldom has to bear the consequences of his or her actions. Someone is always around to bail him or her out.

Often, rebels are the second child of the same sex in a family: a second boy or second girl. In their family, they spent a lot of time defining themselves as different from the older child and fighting for acceptance in their own right. Usually, their sibling was more "approved of" in the family. A younger same sex sibling will often marry someone who is an oldest sibling and proceed to rebel against this authority. The oldest, who was in charge of younger siblings, will gladly try to assert authority over the spouse.

Some relationships can go on for quite a while with one person being the authority and always getting to be right and one person being the rebel and never having to be responsible.

Example

Su-lin, a second sister, married Nickolas, an oldest brother. In many ways they were quite compatible because of her dependency and his willingness to be in charge. But Su-lin didn't like the idea of being dependent. She became something of a feminist and talked about how men hold women back. Yet she never really took any steps to be more self-directing. Though she complained about Nickolas making decisions for her, she kept going along with them. Then he died of a heart attack, and she didn't know what to do with her life. Nickolas had just been a convenient cover for her fear of being a separate, self-sufficient person. Her rebellion was superficial.

QUESTIONS

1. Who was rebellious in your family of origin? How were others affected?

2. What about in your life today? Are you either the authority or a rebel against an authority? What would you be doing with your life if you weren't engaged in this struggle?

2.3 "I'm the king of the mountain" — The attackers

Attackers deal with their anxiety about differences by blaming others for their anxiety as well as for everything else. They know what they want, and are very upset when they don't get it. They think the other is the cause of their frustration and they are not shy about saying that. "If only you would shape up (or be more understanding, or loving, or whatever), then I wouldn't feel so bad." The attacker sees the other as the problem and openly tries to change the other by using whatever means possible.

A relationship in which both partners are attackers resounds to the sound of battle. The attacks and counterattacks are almost continuous as each partner attempts to demonstrate superiority or, at a minimum, equality with the other in all things. It doesn't matter what the topic of argument is; it could be as simple as what movie to see. Unless one does it or sees it or understands it in the same way, the other feels put down. A huge expenditure of energy goes into getting the other to cry uncle.

Example

Donna and Geoff were in almost constant conflict over their differences in matters of taste. For example, Donna liked classical music and intellectual books. Geoff liked rock music and mysteries. They never lost an opportunity to take a jab at each other. Geoff accused Donna of snobbishness and elitism. Donna accused Geoff of being stupid and plastic. They were both, of course, anxious about their differences because they feared the disapproval of the other, so they worked hard at trying to convince the other of the "rightness" of their likes and dislikes.

During therapy, as they each began to feel more comfortable with their own values, they felt less of a need to insist that the other share those values. They were eventually able to acknowledge that they were just different, and there was no right or wrong. Once they accepted the differences, they were better able to negotiate. For example, they took turns deciding which radio station to have on in the car without criticizing the choice of the other. Without the personal attacks, they came to resolutions much more quickly and without either of them feeling attacked.

I'm the king of the mountain

People engaged in such a power struggle often think the other has to change before they can change. They get caught up in a circle of hostility, where each one's "bad" behavior justifies the other's "bad" behavior. He says to her, "I wouldn't drink so much if you didn't nag so much." She says, "I wouldn't nag so much if you didn't drink so much." Somebody has got to stop first to end this impossible situation.

Part of the underlying problem with the attackers is their low self-esteem. Consciously or unconsciously, neither partner feels very good about himself or herself; each wants the other one to make him or her feel better. Of course, a person under attack isn't able to be very giving, so the strategy is self-defeating.

Example

Bette and Azeem blamed each other for the problems in their marriage. Each thought he or she was doing it "right" and the other was doing it "wrong." It didn't matter what the issue was, large or small: which way to drive to grandma's, where to go on vacation, who spent the most money. Each could give an elaborate diagnosis of where the other was at fault.

They decided to try marriage counseling, but each went to get the other one fixed up.

The therapist's questions about family background and past experiences were initially treated as irrelevant and unnecessary since neither Bette nor Azeem thought their own family background was a problem. However, both could see clearly how the other's family background was a problem and became enthusiastic about analyzing the other family and its strangeness. When Bette and Azeem finally explored their own experiences and feelings in their family of origin, they saw how their patterns in their marriage had developed in their families. They realized they each had a fragile self-esteem and were super-sensitive to any criticism from significant others. As they began to take more responsibility for their own feelings and expected less from the other, their power struggles decreased, although they sometimes fought over who was doing the best job of changing!

QUESTIONS

1. Who was involved in overt power struggles in your family? How did the power struggles get started? How did they end?

2. Are you involved in any power struggles today? What else could you do rather than attack and counterattack? What is it that hooks you into the fight?

2.4 "Bye-bye" — The cutoff

For some people, the only way to deal with demands of any kind is to leave or cut off. They withdraw, either physically or emotionally, when things get too tense for them. They can be as subtle as tuning out of a conversation and turning on the TV or as dramatic as leaving the house, the city, or the country. Many people can live in the same house and still be thousands of miles away emotionally.

One version of the cutoff is the man who continues to live with his wife and appears to be in a compliant position, but in fact is emotionally not there. Another version is the young adult who moves away from home and makes duty visits only when it is absolutely essential or unavoidable. That's what Sue, whose story we started with, did in order to avoid her contentious father, even though she was a capable adult during most of the time of her cutoff.

Those who cut off usually do so because they feel powerless. They think the other person has all the power, and they don't see any way to be themselves in a close relationship with that powerful person. They are so unsure of themselves that they deny their need of the other by isolating themselves. These people often appear to be very independent, but like the rebels, it is only a facade. Their independence depends on maintaining emotional distance. They cannot be close without experiencing a great deal of anxiety. They normally function quite well socially and occupationally, perhaps even brilliantly, as long as they do not get emotionally involved. The greater the degree of unresolved emotional attachment in the family of origin, the greater the emotional cutoff can be. Those being cut off also feel powerless and think the person withdrawing has all the power. They don't see any way to be themselves in a close relationship with that person.

Example

After 20 years of marriage Evita and Hernando began to have increasing conflict, mostly because of changes in Evita. For 17 years of their marriage, Hernando had been the master. He used his authoritarian style as a way to cut off from emotional involvement with Evita, the way he had cut off from his family of origin to protect himself from their criticism. Even though he looked superindependent and autonomous, especially in comparison to Evita, he was very dependent underneath. As long as he was distant and in control of his partner he was able to avoid feeling anxious. As long as Evita complied submissively, the relationship worked for him. But Evita stopped being so compliant and finally told him that she was going to leave him. When he found he could not intimidate her into staying, he fell apart. He pleaded with her and told her he couldn't live without her, that she was the most important thing in his life.

The dependency Hernando had never really learned to deal with in his family of origin continued to be an issue for him in his marriage.

Emotional cutoff from the family of origin is a common pattern. We think that by cutting off from the family, we will be free of their power and influence over us and our problems will be over. Of course, what happens is that all those unresolved issues follow us into our new relationships. The clearest example of this is in today's serial marriages and relationships where people keep trying with new partners, but are unsuccessful at developing a satisfying relationship. And it's always the new partner's "fault."

QUESTIONS

1. Who cut off in your family of origin? Was either parent cut off from part or all of their family? What happened to cause the cutoff? How do others in the family react to the cutoff? In what way might the cutoff have affected your own development?

2. Are you cut off from some part of your family? How does the cutoff help or hinder you?

When the natural differences between people in a family become too threatening, one or more family members start to demand sameness. Unless one has developed a strong sense of self, the usual response is to react in one of the four ways just described. In contrast, a healthy, well-functioning family can tolerate many differences between family members. They think the differences are interesting and positive and use them for mutual stimulation and growth rather than fear them.

Chapter 5

HOW TO BE TRUE TO YOURSELF AND STILL HAVE FRIENDS

When I was young, I set out to change the world. When I grew a little older, I perceived that this was too ambitious so I set out to change my state. This, too, I realized as I grew older was too ambitious, so I set out to change my town. When I realized I could not even do this, I tried to change my family. Now as an old man, I know that I should have started by changing myself. If I had started with myself, maybe then I would have succeeded in changing my family, the town, or even the state — and who knows, maybe even the world!

— Words of a Chassidic rabbi on his deathbed

1. FREE TO BE ME — BEING YOURSELF AND KNOWING WHO THAT IS

Br'er Rabbit, in the Joel Chandler Harris story of the old South, walks along the road of life, whistling and happy, until he encounters a "tar baby" on the side of the road who insults him. Br'er Rabbit reacts by striking out at the tar baby. His hand gets stuck in the tar; he tries hitting and kicking some more, and finally he is completely embroiled in all the tar. He had thought he was being himself by not letting someone say nasty things about him. But actually he lost sight of his own goals and got stuck by reacting to someone else's evaluation of him.

It is the same with people. The more we react to others, the more we lose touch with our own goals and become caught in other people's agendas for us. The ability to be close to others and yet not become enmeshed in their opinions, wants, and evaluations is the sign of an emotionally mature person. Therapists call it being differentiated, like a cell that separates itself from another cell, but stays in contact.

To be able to identify and pursue what you want for yourself (i.e., to be yourself) while maintaining a close relationship with others is one of the major goals of family of origin work. Most of us are able to do only one of these things at a time. We either conform in order to be close, or cut off in order to be ourselves.

It is easy enough to be yourself when you are with someone who wants what you want. The difficulties emerge when one person wants something different from the other. Every family and couple struggles with this need for sameness opposed to the need to be an individual. As shown in the last chapter, when one person's demands for sameness begin to infringe on the other's sense of individuality, there is usually a reaction.

Sue, whose story was told in the first chapter, tried to be compliant as a young girl. Then she became a rebellious teen, and later had a power struggle with her parents and told them how they ought to be. Finally she cut off.

No matter what strategy she used, she really was not on the road to being her own person, even when she cut off. When she cut off from her family of origin, she carried all the same feelings into her relationship with Steve. He did the same with her and they both repeated the same struggles they had had in their separate families.

Well-differentiated people are able to be themselves, to do and say what they want, think, and feel without undue concern about whether others will like them or criticize them, and without a need to either flatter or criticize others inappropriately. They can be open about themselves and accept the differences of others without reacting when others try to get them to change in some way. Yet they are open-minded about the possibility of change and are able to rethink their position when new information comes in. They do not think change is an admission of inadequacy.

In order to live a full, happy life, we all need to be able to be this way, particularly with our parents and siblings. The extent to which we are unable to be this way with our families is the extent to which we are still not free from their control.

No one is completely differentiated; the perfect person does not exist. We all go through times of being more or less differentiated in our relationships. But the more often we are able to differentiate, the easier it becomes. Some of the attributes of the well-differentiated person are discussed below.

1.1 Being goal-directed

Being goal-directed means that you are able to clarify your own values and decide what is important to you. You are able to live in a way that is truly expressive of yourself — your wants, beliefs, and values — whether in relationships, work, or other pursuits. You are able to express yourself in spite of being different from intimate others. This does not mean you aggressively attack others or use your own values to put them down. Nor does it mean always saying exactly what you think all the time, regardless of the feelings of others. It just means being able to choose how you want to be: You are not controlled by the approval or disapproval of others.

Being goal-directed does not mean that you do not care about relationships. In fact, relationships can be much more enjoyable when you feel free to be yourself with others. Typically, the goal-directed person has quite good, meaningful, and close relationships and encounters fewer problems in maintaining intimate relationships.

In contrast to the goal-directed person is the relationship-oriented person, who is less emotionally mature. These people depend exclusively on others to provide them with a sense of worth and self-esteem. Their time and energy is spent seeking approval in relationships rather than setting and seeking their own goals.

It is crucial for them that people like and care for them, and it is catastrophic when people don't. Unfortunately, these people often assume people don't care for them. They are obsessed with getting approval and praise, with loving and being loved. They are overly sensitive and can see signs of rejection in even minor differences between themselves and loved ones.

Example

Gina says to her husband, "Aren't those trees lovely?" and he replies, "They're okay." She takes that as a sign that he doesn't love her because he doesn't like what she likes. She criticizes him for being so negative and for not trying to make the marriage a happy experience. Later, he spends a long time doing a house repair she wanted him to do. He thought she would be really happy with his work and thank him, but her first comment is a question about whether he couldn't have done it over to the right a few inches. He immediately reacts with anger saying she never appreciates anything he does and he is not going to do anything for her again!

QUESTIONS

1. How well are you able to be yourself and also be close to others? Are there aspects of your personality that you hide from some people in your life because you think they would dislike you for them? To what extent are your actions dependent on the reactions of others?

2. Who in your family is very different from you? Can you be yourself with that person?

3. Are you more relationship-oriented or goal-directed? What about others in your family?

1.2 Distinguishing between thinking and feeling

Well-differentiated people carefully consider the pros and cons of various choices. They are able to make rational decisions because they distinguish between their thoughts and feelings. They do not insist that others live by their beliefs and they are less likely to become either defensive or aggressive with someone who has different beliefs.

Being differentiated does not mean being unfeeling. Well-differentiated people never lose touch with their feelings, and they can experience and express feelings when necessary. They recognize feelings as one source of information about what is going on in their lives. They can also be passionate in their feelings if they choose. The critical element in a well-differentiated person is this choice. They can decide whether or not to act on feelings.

To be differentiated does not mean to be void of emotion. Differentiated people are able to lose themselves in emotions when they choose. One example is lovemaking, which involves immersing oneself in a world of sensation and feeling and letting go of boundaries.

Because differentiated people think through their positions, they are able to take a stand and set their limits while also listening to the views of others. They are neither wishy-washy nor dogmatic. They can be open to new information, but they are not swayed by threats or emotional blackmail. At the same time they do not condemn those who don't see things as they do. They respect others and learn from them. They can, in fact, delight in differences rather than be threatened by them. Most important, they are able to do this with the people they are closest to: spouse, parents, and children.

People who are not well-differentiated are unable to make the distinction between thinking and feeling. They may be able to perform well in the work world, or when performing thing-oriented tasks, as opposed to people-oriented tasks, but such careful functioning is totally lost when dealing with intimate relationships. They are extremely sensitive and easily hurt. For the sake of the relationship, many make compromises that they would not make if they felt more secure about their identity.

Since they have difficulty distinguishing between thoughts and feelings, less well-differentiated people often assume their subjective feelings are an accurate reflection of the actual state of things. For example, a person like this might say, "I feel that you reject me." But this statement is not about a feeling. It is an interpretation about someone else's behavior. Whenever the word "that" follows the word "feel," a thought is being expressed, not a feeling. Feelings are always about yourself; they cannot be about someone else. A statement about feeling would be, "When you don't agree with me, I feel rejected."

Our feelings are created by the thoughts we have about situations or the interpretations we make about the meaning of what is going on. No one is able to make us feel anything, short of actually physically touching us. All other feelings are created entirely by ourselves. For example, if Joe hits Bill on the shoulder, Bill has a physical sensation of pain. In this case, Joe creates a feeling in Bill. But if Joe says, "I am so angry at you I could hit you," but doesn't actually do it, Bill's feelings about those words are totally up to him. What he feels depends on what he believes Joe is saying. If Bill believes that Joe is so angry that he will hit hard and break a bone or seriously injure him, then Bill might feel fear and run away. If Bill thinks, "Joe is angry, so that means he doesn't like me and that is awful," he might feel hurt and act depressed. If Bill thinks, "No one gets away with being angry at me. Joe can't scare me," he might feel anger himself and perhaps hit Joe first. If Bill thinks, "Well, something really got Joe upset. I wonder what it was?" he might simply feel curious and say, "Tell me more about why you're upset. I'd like to try to work it out with you."

You can see how many different interpretations are possible in one simple situation. A less well-differentiated person will believe that Joe made him have the one particular feeling he has. He will totally discount the role his own interpretation plays in creating his feelings and say that Joe made him feel scared, hurt, angry, or whatever.

A differentiated person, however, will be aware of the many possible interpretations of Joe's anger and will respond, if at all, with curiosity and an invitation to talk about it.

Throughout the process of growing up, we create and adopt beliefs and attitudes toward ourselves and others. Our experiences in our families of origin determine our ideas about what we can, or have to, be in this world, in our relationships, etc. These beliefs then become the basis for all our emotional reactions. Again, our families do not make us have certain beliefs and feelings, no matter how much they may want to. Each of us develops our own unique perception in response to a combination of things like sibling position (see Chapter 7), our parents' experiences in their families of origin, certain biological givens, and many totally unpredictable and indefinable qualities.

We create our own personalities and our own feelings, which means that we have the power to change them. We don't have to wait for others to change before we decide to change.

Try the following exercise to distinguish between thinking statements and feeling statements.

THINKING AND FEELING

How often in a day do you say the words, "I feel that … " when you are really expressing an opinion, not a feeling. Try to catch yourself doing it and change the statement to "I think that … " What is the change like for you?

Notice how often you and those around you say things like "that makes me feel awful," "you really upset me," "you make me sick," etc. What is a more accurate way of describing these subjective experiences? Start saying it that way and see if people respond differently.

---

2. STUCK IN THE MESS — FUSION

The opposite of differentiation is fusion. To be fused is to be stuck in the tar of a symbiotic or parasitic relationship. It means that you are always reacting to others in one way or another. Any version of the four basic reactive strategies described in Chapter 4 (compliance, rebellion, attack, cutoff) is an expression of fusion.

Example

Margareta and Paolo were caught in a power struggle. No matter what the topic — politics, religion, children, household chores — each had a totally different understanding of it. They each accused the other of being wrong on every topic and saw their differences as the problem. However, they were very much the same. Both were quite dependent in spite of their apparent independence in thought and actions. Margareta was threatened when Paolo disagreed with her because she needed his support. Paolo felt rejected when Margareta would not do things his way. Each wanted more closeness, but only on their own terms. When Paolo was asked what "closeness" meant, he immediately responded that he thought of it as "being like a mother and baby" (the model of a fused relationship) where "the mother would be so sensitive to the needs of the baby that those needs would be met without any request ever being made. When people are close, they just know intuitively what the other wants and they do it." This is what he wanted from Margareta, and she from him. Their battles were an attempt to make each other into the ideal nurturing figure.

Paolo's definition of closeness is what many of us mean by "love." But it is an example of fusion. The relationship between mother and infant begins as a fused one. But growing up means becoming a separate, distinct, self-supporting person responsible for meeting your own needs.

It is difficult even for adults to give up that need for oneness. Our dream is to find that special person who will give us this kind of love in an intimate relationship. When we fall in love, we think we have found that person. As soon as we find out that we were mistaken, we start complaining about the lack of communication. What most people mean by "communication," however, is sameness. When people think they are "really communicating," they usually mean they are thinking about things in the same way. When Margareta says Paolo is not communicating, the problem really is that he is not communicating what she wants communicated. We are always communicating; we can't not communicate. So when Paolo's wants are different from Margareta's wants, he may deal with it by distancing and becoming involved with work (while wishing she understood him better and would be more like him), and she may deal with it by pushing for closeness and intimacy (meaning sameness) and wanting him to "communicate." Both are dealing with unresolved emotional attachments in their families of origin; they are trying to achieve the blissful state of togetherness they had hoped marriage would provide.

Fusion is a very powerful element in relationships. People can come to know each other almost as well as they know themselves. They can know the wants and wishes, thoughts and feelings of the other without the other ever saying a word.

People who are "intuitive" are experts at this process. They usually grew up in a relatively fused family where being able to sense moods and feelings was essential to their well-being. However, intuitive people are usually also reactive; they constantly monitor their standing with others and check out how others feel about them now, and determine their own behavior in response to what they think others want, think, or feel. They may not even know what they want for themselves, much less be able to say it.

In highly fused families, the differences between family members are denied, and many of the unspoken rules described in Chapter 2 control behavior in the family. One test of fusion in a family is how easily someone can say, "Hey, this seems to be going on in our family" (identifying a rule) and then talk about it with other family members. The more fused family will refuse to acknowledge that the rule exists and won't talk about it. Many families can continue indefinitely in this state and never change. Some change when one member of the family develops enough self-esteem to be able to risk being different and deal with the reactions that provokes. Other families are forced to change, or at least to become aware of problems, when their children become adolescents.

Adolescence is the time when both the spoken and unspoken family rules get tested and challenged. In fused families, it is the time when things start to fall apart. The need for separateness becomes more pressing in the child than the need for togetherness. Parents often complain that they had a perfect child who was always obedient, did well in school, etc., until around the ages of 13 to 16. They mean that the child had been fulfilling their expectations. They become anxious as differences begin to emerge and the child pursues his or her own wants. Often, at least one parent will deal with the differences and resulting anxiety by controlling and punishing the child frequently. This works with some, but it only puts off the time of separating ("I'll wait until I leave home") and leads to more cutoff when the child does leave. The child thinks, "I can't be myself at home so I won't go back there much."

The more fusion in the family, the more the child feels threatened by that fusion and tries to break it by moving away emotionally. The more control the parents impose at this time, the greater the battles. The adolescent will end up doing things that outrage the parents as a way of demonstrating that he or she is different and cannot be controlled by the parents.

Example

Richard was the head of the household. There was an unspoken rule to never challenge his authority. Everyone compliantly recognized this rule until Annie, the youngest girl, turned 13. For many reasons, Annie refused to recognize the rule any more and became quite rebellious toward her father. Richard complained, "She wants to take over my place at the head of the table." Her refusal to comply with his authority hit him and the family at its most vulnerable place. She was identified by the family as a troublemaker and taken into therapy with the request to fix her up and make her obedient again. Because her rebellion provoked a great deal of anxiety in her father and in the rest of the family, it was identified by the family as deviant. Eventually the family was able to talk about this issue and Richard's uneasiness about his authority and how this affected his relationship with his wife. In fact, Annie's behavior reflected some of her mother's deep feelings of resentment toward Richard, which she had been afraid to admit to herself. Annie's "problem" ended up leading to a helpful change in the family. But it doesn't always end this happily.

The difficulty with rebellious behavior is that it does not represent true independence. Even the most cocky kid is suffering from low self-esteem and is still fused and very much controlled by the parents, but reacting by doing the opposite of what the parents want. The rebellious adolescent is not thinking independently or setting his or her own goals. In fact, the rebellion is often self-destructive.

Frequently, when adolescents rebel in highly fused families, they establish an equally intense fused relationship with their peers and become very much like them. Again the need for sameness and togetherness takes over, and they have a great deal of difficulty differentiating themselves in this new group. The group's basic purpose is to rebel against parental and other authority. In the process of doing this, the adolescents provide each other with mutual support and nurture, but only for the act of rebelling, rarely for differentiating.

Example

Savita, a 15-year-old in a highly fused family, was a "model child" until seventh grade when she began to rebel against her parents' authority. She then became equally fused with a group of older kids and did increasingly outrageous things in an attempt to win their approval. However, this backfired and all she got was a bad reputation. So she changed schools and became involved with another undifferentiated and needy boy; she tried to save him with her love and excessive nurturing. This was also destructive for her. By the age of 18 she felt that her life was over and she was considering suicide. In therapy, Savita was able to look at her low self-esteem and fusion needs, and she began the process of differentiating from parents and peers and making her own decisions based on what was good for her.

Savita: then and now

1. Think of two situations where your family success-fully dealt with differences between its members, and two situations where the outcome was not successful. What kind of process did each family member (including you) go through in attempting to deal with these differences?

2. Remember some times in your family when a rule was identified, discussed, and possibly changed. What was the impact of this experience on the family?

3. YOU MADE ME DO IT — BEING RESPONSIBLE FOR YOURSELF

A crucial element in the functioning of less differentiated families is confusion over who is responsible for what. And that doesn't mean who is supposed to wash the dishes. It means that family members believe one person can make another person feel something.

The more differentiated the family, the more all members take responsibility for their own feelings, thoughts, and behavior and recognize that each person is the originator of those experiences. When people in the family are able to do this, they start talking in a different way about their problems. They are comfortable saying the literal truth, "I am angry," rather than shifting attention to others by saying, "You made me angry."

In fused families, as children relate to parents (even if the children are adults themselves), they become sensitive to certain issues and stay away from discussion of these areas because "it will make Mom or Dad feel bad." The more fused the family, the greater the number of issues that will upset family members. The rationale for avoiding them is to keep from upsetting someone.

However, because we usually feel upset, too, when someone else gets upset, the real motive is self-protection. We don't "upset" them so they won't "upset" us. This is what usually happens in times of peace in fused families; people avoid dealing with and talking about differences because that could be an upsetting experience. They play-act at being the same and thus keep the peace. Then, when things begin to get tense in the family and the pressure for togetherness and sameness begins to feel uncomfortable, they lose this self-control and accuse others by implying or saying directly, "It's your fault that I am this way (e.g., angry, sad) and if only you would change I could be happy." They then state the other person's problem — the topic being avoided before — and say it is the cause of their problem.

One example of this is the husband who says, "I can't feel free and at ease in social situations because you are so critical of what I say." By saying that, he is trying to make his wife responsible for his own uneasiness or insecurity, rather than examining how he can be less sensitive to her criticism (if, in fact, she really is critical).

The battle to change the other person is never won. Taking responsibility for yourself means that you work on changing yourself, not someone else.

People who are completely dependent on another person for love and approval will inevitably feel pressure to be and act the way the other wants in order to maintain that love and approval. However, this process of trading off being ourselves to win acceptance eventually breaks down. Either we get angry at the other person (often about some unrelated thing) or we take it out on ourselves in some self-destructive way, such as depression. True acceptance means accepting the differences, so we are accepted only when we are truly ourselves. At some level, we are aware of any false acceptance and resentful of it.

Hiding your true self from someone to avoid upsetting that person saves some pain and hurt in the short run, but it guarantees confusion and battles, or worse, over the long run.

QUESTIONS

1. Can you identify some basic beliefs you have developed in your family of origin that are creating upsetting experiences for you now?

2. What are some topics or issues that were avoided in your family because people became upset when they were raised? What impact has this agreement to ignore a significant issue had on you and your family life?

3. Are there any ways people have traded off their own beliefs in your family of origin for the sake of approval?

4. When you come home at the end of the day and your partner is in a bad mood, while you are in a

good mood, how long does it take for your mood to begin to turn sour? Have you ever been able to delay or change that?

---

4. LET MOTHER TAKE CARE OF IT — UNDER-FUNCTIONING AND OVER-FUNCTIONING

The dynamic of under-functioning and over-functioning operates in almost every relationship. One person appears more responsible, more capable, and generally healthier than the other. Usually, it looks as though one is merely more mature than the other. However, if a long-term under-functioning person improves, the over-functioning person often begins to deteriorate and perform less well. When one is up, the other is down. An apparently normal husband will get depressed when his wife begins to come out of a depression; an apparently functional wife will stop functioning when her husband comes out of a manic state; a husband will begin to experience premature ejaculation when his wife loses her frigidity and becomes interested in sex.

The same thing happens when there is improvement in a "problem" adolescent; the over-involved, over-functioning parent begins to cease functioning as well and becomes more anxious and upset.

4.1 Negative consequences

In unhealthy relationships, the roles become frozen into more or less permanent positions of over- and under-functioning. The over-functioner may appear, for example, to be taking care of both, and the under-functioner may appear to be totally dependent and fused in the relationship. But, in fact, each may be at a similarly low level of differentiation. The over-functioner is dependent on the under-functioner and vice versa.

Whenever someone in a relationship is acting as the under-functioner, someone else is sure to be doing an equal amount of over-functioning. Over-functioning and under-functioning go hand in hand; one cannot happen without the other.

Under- and over-functioners are involved in fused relationships. One takes the responsibility and the other makes or lets the other take it. One tends to be seen as good and the other as bad, but, in fact, they are both cooperating to keep the situation as it is. Each loses this way.

The over-functioner tends to feel that there is no option but to take on the responsibility and do the work required. He or she thinks the other is totally incapable of functioning in this area and feels forced to do it. Even the over-functioner who thinks the other is manipulating him or her into doing it still feels there is no choice. The over-functioner may even angrily accuse the other of willfully avoiding the responsibility ("you are just too lazy"), but still feel obligated to do the job and take on responsibility for the other ("someone has to do it"). The under-functioner may actually feel incapable and so allow, or even expect, the other to be responsible. In this case, the most frequently used phrase of the under-functioner is "I can't."

Example

Al, a perfectly normal, intelligent, mechanically-minded man was asked by his partner to take responsibility for doing the family laundry. He replied, "I don't know how to run the washing machine. I can't figure out which clothes take the permanent press cycle. All those dials confuse me, etc." For a while that worked, and his partner continued to do all the household tasks. Finally, it got to the point where Al's partner refused to be the over-functioner any longer. Al's laundry did not get done; he quickly learned how to use the machine.

Under-functioners can plead any number of reasons why they aren't able to handle something, but one of their favorites is illness. Sick people don't have as much expected of them; they are excused from the normal burdens of life. They also get a lot of attention and have considerable control over what happens in the family. Others in the family change their lives in order to make allowances for the sick person. The whole family may organize itself around the sick person, whether the sickness is physical or emotional.

In other cases, where the under-functioners think they would like to do more, they may see the over-functioners as controlling or dominating. Then the favorite phrase is, "You won't let me."

Example

Jenny always complained, "I'd love to go out and get a job and earn my own money, but my husband won't let me." In this case, though at odds with each other overtly, it became clear that they were helping each other avoid something. She was protecting his self-esteem as the breadwinner; if he felt threatened she would begin to feel insecure. He was protecting her from her fear of being inadequate in the work world. But each blamed the other and made the other responsible for their own anxiety.

4.2 Positive consequences

In healthy relationships, there is also over- and under-functioning to the extent that the two people operate as a team, but the roles constantly change back and forth and never become frozen. Both partners are aware of and consent to the changes. Each agrees to let the other be in charge in certain areas and at certain times, and both can step out of the roles whenever they choose without any sense of blame, hostility, or defensiveness.

Example

Kim and Kikuo had fallen into a routine where Kim assumed the responsibility for their joint social lives. They were aware that they had both assigned this role to Kim and both were happy with it for many years. Gradually, however, Kim began to tire of the responsibility and Kikuo began to feel programmed to death. So they talked it over and decided that it was time for Kikuo to be in charge of making, or not making, social engagements for them as a couple.

Try this exercise to examine your level of over or under-functioning.

DETERMINE YOUR FUNCTIONAL LEVEL

Examine the areas of your life in which you are being the over- or under-functioner. As a short-term experiment (perhaps for a week), change your functioning level in one area to the opposite of what you are now doing.

What happens to the anxiety level in each of you as you do this? What other issues emerge between the two of you (which were previously hidden) as you change your functional level?

---

5. CONCLUSION

Let's look at a typical scene in a marriage to see how all these issues can come together in one simple interchange.

Example

Joe and Nancy are getting ready for a dinner party. As the time to leave gets closer, Nancy is increasingly uneasy. She tries on several dresses and doesn't like any of them, but ends up with what she thinks is the best of the lot. As she is putting on her final touches of makeup, Joe walks in. In frustration she blurts out, "I just look awful! I don't know what to wear." Joe, as is his usual style when Nancy is upset, fails to hear her underlying request for reassurance and in his normal businesslike, problem-solving style, thinking she wants advice on what to wear, suggests, "Why don't you wear your green dress? That blue dress does look kind of dowdy." Nancy, now angry at him for failing to read her mind correctly, says, "Oh, you make me sick! I bet you won't say that about the low-cut dress Mary will probably wear tonight! Why don't you just go without me? You'll probably spend the whole evening with her anyway!" Joe, feeling frustrated that his good intentions were totally misunderstood, comes back in anger, "God, are you starting this again? We haven't even got there yet! You make me so angry! What's the matter with you?" They have a few more exchanges like this, each trying to point out how the other is wrong. Finally, Nancy falls apart in tears. Joe's anger then melts. He goes over and puts his arms around her and says he was just trying to help. She explains that that wasn't the kind of help she wanted and tells him what she did want. He then reassures her that she looks just fine. She hugs him closer and kisses him. He begins to think she's feeling sexy and moves her toward the bed. Again, feeling misunderstood, she pushes him away and says, "Is that all you can think of? You have a one-track mind." He retorts that no wonder he is interested in Mary's low-cut dress since he has such an "uptight, frigid wife," and they are back to accusing each other of various evils. It ends up with Joe stomping out of the bedroom and slamming the door.

Nearly all of the dynamics discussed in Chapters 3, 4, and 5 are portrayed in this example. Joe and Nancy struggle with conflicting needs for closeness and distance. Nancy looks for closeness by asking to be reassured. Joe looks for closeness through sexual contact. When they begin to think that being close means doing or being what the other wants and not getting what they want, they both withdraw. They handle their anxiety or sense of threat by using at least three of the four styles of reacting to the pressure for sameness. The power struggle is the most dominant, but Joe was slightly compliant in response to Nancy's tears, and he cut off when he left the room. They are fused in that each sees the other as the cause of their own feelings and mood. If only he/she were different, they think, I'd be okay. They each think the other is being purposely selfish and unkind. At the same time, both are quite sensitive to the other's evaluations. Both try to make their own self-esteem the other's responsibility. Nancy was on the verge of under-functioning by asking Joe what she should wear and Joe was ready to be the over-functioner by telling her.

Learning to be emotionally mature involves identifying how we function in situations like this and changing our perceptions and actions where appropriate.

Chapter
6

TRIANGLES IN RELATIONSHIPS

All the world's a stage

And all the men and women merely players.

They have their exits and their entrances,

And one man in his time plays many parts.

— William Shakespeare, *As You Like It*

When Sue was young, she often saw her parents arguing. Her dad got red-faced and shouted at her mother. Her mother cried and gave in to him. Sue felt sorry for Mother and angry at Dad. After Dad stormed out of the room, Sue tried to comfort her mother.

As Sue got older, her mother told her about other incidents of her father's mistreatments. In her teens, Sue began to fight back with Dad in a way mother never would. She was especially incensed whenever Dad attacked her brothers and sisters. Those fights would then take a back seat to the fight between Dad and Sue. Eventually, in her last years at home, Sue began to see that her mother's inability to speak up for herself was part of the problem. She then got angry at Mother and called her a wimp whenever she didn't stand up for herself. Mother would cry and Dad would tell Sue to stop being mean to her mother. Then Sue and her dad would be fighting again.

Sue and her family were caught up in a common relationship game called triangles. Unless you can anticipate the power of triangles and understand their functioning in your own family, your attempts to change will be defeated.

1. THREE'S A CROWD — WHAT IS A TRIANGLE ANYWAY?

Basically, a triangle is any three-way relationship. In each corner there can be an individual or a group of people. The basic family triangle is father, mother, child. A basic social triangle might be criminal, victim, police. The classic triangle everyone knows of, and probably thinks of when they hear the word, is husband, wife, mistress. One corner of a triangle can also be a thing, or an activity, or an issue. As many wives say, "My husband's work is his mistress."

The triangle is the main dynamic on TV soap operas. All the drama and frustration of these shows is created by people not saying things directly to each other. The characters give their information, or pass on gossip, to a third party, rather than to the person directly involved. Watch soap operas with this perspective and you will see how easy it is for people to make a mess of their lives, and how accurately these shows reflect this aspect of our own lives.

Triangles have both positive and negative functions. As mentioned in Chapter 3, people in relationships have optimal levels of closeness and distance. Anxiety arises when there is either too much closeness or too much distance. If there are a lot of people around, the anxiety can be diluted. This means there is more potential stability available in large families. When one person gets too anxious, he or she can go to someone else in the family for a while until things cool down and then come back to the original relationship. For example, when a parent and child got into unmanageable conflict in our grandparents' generation, the child would be sent to live with an uncle or aunt in the neighboring community. Each party had a chance to think things through, get some ideas from others and then, perhaps, renew the relationship on different terms. Most families today are too scattered geographically and emotionally to do this.

Today's nuclear family is like a pressure cooker; there are very few places, other than a therapist's office, where family members can go to learn how to deal with anxiety. And because so many people believe that they ought to be able to handle it themselves, the pressure keeps growing until the family explodes. More people, and more triangles, in the family could ease this tension.

However, in most families, triangles increase rather than reduce the problems. Triangles occur because it is usually difficult for any two people in a relationship to focus just on themselves and maintain a one-to-one relationship. The less differentiated they are, the less they are able to do this.

In a one-to-one relationship, the tension usually grows. People handle this tension by triangling in a third person or issue and talk about that. They can continue in the relationship that way for hours, days, weeks, and years. Some couples get along fine as long as they talk about their kids, or their friends, or their work, but they have trouble focusing on themselves in the relationship. In Sue's case, she later learned that her mother had run home to her own mother (Sue's maternal grandmother) several times during the first year of marriage after conflicts with her husband. She had complained to her mother that he was mean to her and her mother told her, "Men are like that. They are insensitive brutes and nothing can be done. That is just one of the burdens wives have to bear." Then she was sent back home to do her wifely duties. Sue's mother felt powerless in an unchangeable situation. Her mother was unable to provide her with any additional resources for dealing with her husband and in a negative kind of way sided with him.

Another mother might have said, "I told you he was wrong for you. You stay here with me and I'll take care of you." They would have traded stories about the husband which proved he was really a bad person and didn't deserve the daughter for a wife. After a while, when conflicts with the mother surfaced, the daughter would remember why she wanted to get away from home and mother in the first place. She had left one dominant person for another.

Yet another mother could have just listened and helped Sue's mother talk about her feelings about herself, shared stories of her own struggles in marriage, and then let Sue's mother make up her own mind about what to do.

In any group of three people there will tend to be two who are close (inside) and one who is distant (outside). It is difficult to maintain equal closeness between all three at the same time. The closeness can rotate so that any one person can be on the outside while the other two are close, or the close two and distant third might be permanently fixed. The usual pattern is that the close two form a coalition against the outside person and overlook their differences with each other. In its mildest forms, this pattern of interaction is called gossip.

The first two situations with the mother above show the negative way triangles operate when there is side-taking. There is little focus on self and instead, the two inside people talk about the outside person. They focus on him or her rather than themselves. When the wife goes back to her husband, they could begin to talk about how controlling her mother is rather than what is wrong between them.

In the third situation, the two inside people are able to focus on themselves more than on the outside person, which leads to more constructive solutions.

To see how long you can maintain a one-to-one focus, try this experiment.

FOCUS ON YOURSELF

Get together with a close friend or your spouse. Sit close, touching knees and maintaining eye contact. See how long you can talk only about yourself or your relationship with the other person, not about a third person or topic. Now, to make it even more difficult, do this while staying totally in the present tense. Do not talk about the past or future, just your experience with each other right now.

Example

When Anna and Bill get together and start talking about Charlene, they frequently act as if they are in agreement about Charlene and her strengths and weaknesses. The implication is that Anna and Bill are alike and, therefore, close because they share the same viewpoints, and that Charlene, being different, is more distant. But when Bill is with Charlene, they act as if they are the same, and therefore, close, and that Anna is distant because different. Charlene and Anna may also get together and talk about Bill's differences. In each case, the difference between the two people in the close relationship is ignored (because that would create anxiety), and they act as if they are in agreement about the third person's differences.

In most relationships, very little time is devoted to talking together about one's self and the other and the relationship. Most time is spent talking about other people or things. It is quite normal, and it is a natural way to keep a balance between closeness and distance in relationships. But if it is the only way people relate, it is likely that a great deal of fusion is going on and differences between the two people are either being ignored or not handled well.

This happens in families, among groups of friends, and in office work groups, as well as at a national and international level. It is one of the negative functions of triangles, but it is a universal way of dealing with the anxiety about closeness and differences.

Remember that the anxiety about closeness has to do with "how close can I be and still be myself, be different, and not have to be or do what the other wants me to be or do?" or "How close can I be and allow the other person to be different from me?"

Closeness works just fine when two people are in agreement, but when their differences emerge, they tend to distance and/or create power struggles. It is at this time that one of them will be tempted to triangle in someone or something else.

One common example of this is when husband and wife are arguing; at some point in the argument one of them triangles in one or more of the kids and says, "And Johnny agrees with me. He thinks you're wrong, too!" The implication is "if we two think you are wrong then you must be wrong and you had better change and be the way we want you to be."

Triangles have two different states: calm and tense. In the calm state, the triangle consists of two close people who are getting along well and a distant person who would like to be in closer.

In this triangle, the outside person may try to entice one of the close partners to enter a new coalition and leave the other partner. One example is a teenager who feels on the outside of her parents' united front and develops a strategy for playing one off against the other so that one of the parents ends up agreeing with her and fighting her cause with the other parent.

In the tense triangle, the two close people may become anxious over the closeness and potential loss of self and begin a fight. In this case, the outside person usually wants to stay distant and avoid the other two, if possible, while one of the two close members tries to establish a coalition with the outside person.

For example, while the parents are fighting, Dad may try to triangle in a teenage child to be on his side against Mom. The teenager may then try to distance from the argument and say, "Leave me out of this. This is between the two of you."

On the other hand, if the teenager wants more closeness with Dad, she may agree with Dad about Mom and imply that she and Dad are alike and Mom is wrong. In this case her need to be closer to Dad (and perhaps to "get" Mom) overrides her need to distance from these two arguing parents.

QUESTIONS

1. What were (are) the major triangles in your family of origin? List the parties that made up each corner. If you come from a large family, there will probably be quite a few triangles.

2. Think back over the years of your parents' marriage. What was your relationship to each of them? Was it easy to be close with both of them? Only one of them? Neither of them? What happened to your relationship to the outside person when you were close to the other?

3. Usually we are closest to one parent. What would it be like for you to invite the more distant parent to go out to lunch with you alone? What would happen to your relationship with the closer parent? Would this be a problem for you?

2. HOW TRIANGLES OPERATE

Let's take a more extensive look at how triangles can operate in the families shown below. In this family diagram (called a genogram), three generations of parents and children are represented: the two sets of grandparents, Grandpa and Grandma Green, Pops and Nana White; the children from those two sets of parents: Sue, Barb, Chuck, Stan, and Sandi, Calvin, Stu; and the children, Liz and Chuck Jr., of parents Chuck and Sandi. (Men are indicated by squares and women by circles in genograms.)

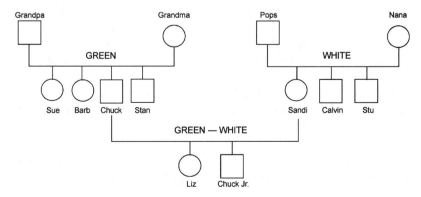

One basic triangle is the three families with one family in each corner: the Greens in one corner; the Whites in another; and the Green-Whites in the third corner. Note that both Chuck and Sandi are the connecting links in the triangles. But the emotional connections and potential coalitions are not limited to these two figures. There are 131 potential three-person triangles in this 13-member extended family and, remembering that each triangle could be experienced from one of three corners, that gives 393 potential positions. On top of that you can add other coalition triangles like an in-law triangle of Grandpa and Grandma in one corner, Chuck in the other, and Sandi in the third corner as in the following example. (The wavy line indicates conflict.)

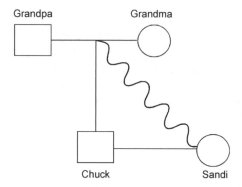

A common triangle is between two parents and a child. For example, for the first two years of their marriage Chuck and Sandi got along very well. They got just the right amount of attention and understanding from each other and a satisfying closeness/distance balance. Then, when Liz was born a new triangle was created and much of Sandi's attention and energy began to be devoted to Liz rather than to Chuck.

It is not possible, when any three people are together, for each to get equal attention and energy devoted to them. Liz got the mothering and nurturing that Chuck had previously received. Chuck, as many fathers do, then began to feel on the outside (the distant position in the triangle), less cared for by Sandi, and resentful toward Liz. He felt silly about being jealous and did not talk to Sandi about this; but he started seeking more satisfaction and attention from others at work (it could have been at church, or at a bar, or with another woman). In the new, secondary triangle, between Chuck's work, and Chuck and Sandi, Sandi felt on the outside and uncared for by Chuck. They each felt rejected by the other and saw a third party (Liz or work) as competition.

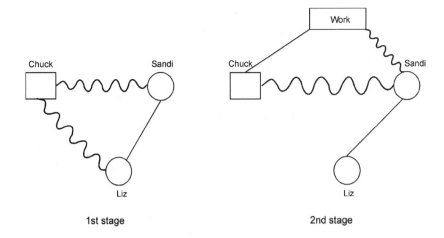

1st stage

2nd stage

Another common triangle is the one called sibling rivalry. As an infant, Liz felt close to her mother and enjoyed her attention. When Liz was three years old, Chuck Jr. was born and began to get much of Mom's attention. Then Sandi and Chuck Jr. had the close, inside relationship, and Liz was in the distant, outside position of the triangle. Liz then started acting like a baby herself to get Mom's attention.

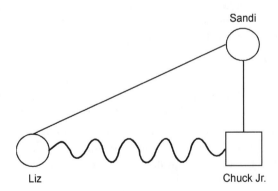

Liz could have tried to get back at Chuck Jr. for coming in to her close twosome, thus creating sibling rivalry for Mom's attention. Or she could have tried to win attention from Dad to compensate for the loss from Mom, which would have created a new triangle between herself, Mom, and Dad.

There are still more typical triangles in this extended family. In the White family, Nana, for whatever reasons, wanted to maintain distance from her husband, Pops. He went along with this and met his needs elsewhere. When Sandi was born, Nana began a long-term process of focusing on, worrying, and being concerned about, and even depending on her daughter. When Calvin and Stu were born, however, she spent less time worrying about them. She thought, "They are boys and they can take care of themselves, just like their dad." As a consequence, it was much harder for Sandi to differentiate from Nana than it was for Calvin and Stu. Sandi had to spend a lot of her time and emotional energy coping with Nana's dependence on her. She did not have the energy available, then, for getting on with her own life. She also felt she had to serve as a substitute parent for the boys and began to see herself as someone who waits on others rather than someone with goals of her own. She was less free than the boys to go her own way because of her sense of obligation. It became very difficult for her to be her own person. In this situation, there was an intense closeness between Nana and Sandi, and the two boys were in the outside position. When things were tense between Nana and Sandi, the boys were happy to be distant, but when Sandi was getting privileges they didn't get, they were envious.

Sandi, trained as an over-functioner, married Chuck, who was an under-functioner in his family and was used to having women wait on him. Sandi related to him the same way she related to Nana's dependence on her by feeling obligated to look after him and do for him what they both thought he couldn't do for himself. As a way to deal with her anxiety over differences, Sandi gave up herself, let go of her own wants, and made sure she took care of Chuck, just as she took care of her mother.

However, Sandi also said to herself, "I'm not going to make my daughter work in the house and be a substitute parent for me the way I had to for my mom. I'm going to let her be a child." So she focused all her attention and energy on Liz rather than on herself, which, paradoxically, was exactly what her own mother did to her. Therefore, it was harder for Liz to differentiate herself from Sandi and be her own person, responsible for herself.

When Liz hit adolescence, Nana was getting older and even more dependent on Sandi. Both Liz and Nana, under-functioners, began making increased demands on Sandi, the over-functioner. She, of course, felt obligated to meet those demands. And yet, as she did so, she became even more aware of losing self and literally having no time for herself. If there had been open hostility between Liz and Nana, or at a minimum, competition for Sandi's time, her job would have been complicated within this triangle by having to be a peacekeeper.

During all this, Sandi's husband, Chuck, started feeling cheated of his wife's affections and thinking that she owed more time and attention to him than she did to her daughter or mother. He regarded Nana as a "controlling, demanding old hag" and Liz as a "manipulative, spoiled little girl." He told Sandi it was all her fault that they were this way and that, furthermore, she gave them more attention than she gave to him out of some kind of spite. This increased Sandi's sense of obligation and the pressures she felt.

Another triangle that developed involved Chuck and Chuck Jr. Chuck wanted to repeat with his son the relationship he had enjoyed with his little brother, Stan, in which he was the boss and ordered Stan around in order to meet his own needs. He also wanted to be a better father to his son than his dad was to him. He and Chuck Jr. did a lot together and developed an intense relationship. Chuck Jr. really enjoyed this relationship with Dad until he became an adolescent and wanted to do things on his own. Then conflict erupted between them as Chuck attempted to hang onto Chuck Jr. and the companionship he had provided.

At that point, each tried to triangle in Sandi to get her support. She already felt the pressure from her other three triangles with Nana and Liz and Chuck. She was then at the apex of a fourth triangle with Chuck and Chuck Jr. She felt pulled in four different directions and obligated to support them all or at a minimum try to keep peace in the family.

Frequently, this kind of situation ends in something that modern society calls a breakdown. Breakdowns are usually the only socially acceptable way that over-functioners can see to get out of being responsible for others. But the hospital stays are only brief respites because people return to the original situation with the same sense of their responsibilities, and the experiences are repeated.

The exercise on the next page will help you focus in on some of the triangles in your family of origin.

3. YOU AND ME AGAINST HER — THE MEANING OF COALITIONS IN TRIANGLES

As mentioned, coalitions between two points of a triangle serve two functions: to reduce anxiety and to control the third point of the triangle. Coalitions provide both additional support and additional strength to a person who is feeling anxious and weak.

YOUR TRIANGLES

Imagine you are sitting in your parents' living room. You and your same sex parent are having a conversation. Then your opposite sex parent comes in and sits down with the two of you. What would happen to your conversation? Are you aware of any physical changes in yourself? What do you feel? Think? What do you want to do? What would you actually do?

Now go through this same exercise imagining that you are having a conversation with your opposite sex parent and the same sex parent comes in.

Do this same fantasy exercise with each member of your family. What happens to you as various third parties walk in on your conversation? Do you feel any strong pulls of loyalty? Do you stay an inside person or become an outside person in the triangle? How does this affect you?

Coalitions are a normal experience in families. The newborn baby is triangled into coalitions before it even has any awareness of itself. But as self-awareness develops, the baby learns how to play the coalition game.

Coalitions help those who feel weak deal with those whom they see as stronger. Those who feel less sure of themselves see their salvation (i.e., their chances of getting their way) in the support of others. Coalitions are an attempt to help us deal with our poor self-esteem and increase our influence.

One example shows how the coalition can help shore up a poor self-image. Many men and women today, from their mid-30s to mid-40s, go through a mid-life crisis. Whatever this really is, it also includes confronting the discrepancy between what we had hoped life would be and what it actually is. Our middle-aged spouse may reflect back to us our own age; our marriage problems and unrealized relationship or career dreams confront us with our failures there. We begin to think that perhaps a new kind of life, a fresh start, with a new and younger partner will help us get back the lost hopes of our younger days, or at least live out our remaining life in a more fulfilling way.

We may then enter into another coalition with an attractive new partner and begin to feel rejuvenated. As is usually the case in coalitions, being with this person makes us feel more attractive, intelligent, witty, sexy, energetic, etc., than we really are. Our spouse, the outside person, is seen only in a negative light.

In coalitions, the inside person is good and attractive and the outside person is bad and unattractive. When we make coalitions, we tend to distort reality. This demonstrates that the real intent of coalitions is to shore up one's sense of self and to get "good things" from others.

Therefore, coalitions become disillusioning, and we end up feeling weaker, or taken advantage of ("He was only after my body." "She was only out for my money").

Some people recognize that this is what it's about before too much damage is done to the marriage relationship and can go back to that relationship to try to work out the problems. It may still end in a divorce, but by facing the issues in that relationship they are also dealing with themselves. They end up feeling stronger in themselves and better about whatever new life they end up putting together, with or without their married partner.

Other people fail to realize what is going on, continue to see their spouse and the new person in black and white terms, and ignore their own role in the situation.

They get divorced and move in with another person only to find they didn't really know her or him at all and that, eventually, they have the same problems with their new partners that they did with their first spouse. Even then some people don't learn there is something to deal with in self and think the problem is just "women" or "men."

Of course, it is true that coalitions do increase strength. Political parties know this. Every little boy who's been beaten up by a bully and gets his older brother to go to school with him the next day knows this. Every wife who feels dominated by her husband, and who has been able to triangle in a child to win an argument with him knows this. In fact, it is not always an advantage to be seen as the strongest person in a family, because others will be provoked into forming coalitions against you.

Example

Eric was very dominating in any one-to-one relationship in his family. He was seen by his wife and two daughters as an absolute tyrant and dictator. And yet when they formed coalitions, he hardly ever got his way and often felt quite frustrated. He dealt with this by trying to buy off different members from time to time with gifts (his only real power was his hold on the money), but these temporary coalitions rarely lasted.

Secret coalitions also develop in families. They are quite difficult to deal with simply because they are not openly acknowledged, so cannot be challenged. They can be quite destructive.

Example

In one family, Father was quite dominating and Mother felt much weaker. When they were together with their son, Mother would always agree with Father in order to present a united front to the boy. Father thought she agreed with him. But when Father was not around, she would communicate her real feelings to the boy and let him do things Father would not let him do, without telling the father. They each got secret pleasure out of this way of beating Father. But, as he got older, the boy started doing things that Mother didn't approve of, and he began lying to her the way they both had lied to Father. Because she needed him so much for support in the relationship against Dad, she let him get away with this. Dad began beating up both the boy and the mother when she came to his rescue. Mother and Father separated, and Mother hoped the boy would now settle down. But instead, he began doing exactly what he wanted to. At the age of 15, he came and went as he pleased and ended up with serious criminal problems. She never was able to establish effective limits on his behavior, essentially because she still had not changed in her feelings about her own strength. Without a coalition, she felt powerless.

Another common coalition is between parents and "the good child" against "the bad child." The bad child will always be in the outside position. The good child is in coalition with the parents, because he or she overtly does what they want or emulates their values, and thus is seen (as is the case in coalitions) as almost all good. And the bad child is, of course, seen as almost all bad. Frequently, in therapy, the good child, now grown up, will say that he or she did nearly all the same things as the bad sibling but never got caught and that the parents seemed to think he or she could do no wrong. This is often the situation when one child is being scapegoated (i.e., when one child is blamed for being the source of all the family's problems).

The scapegoat phenomenon is common in all groups. It is a normal way to handle anxiety, and it can be observed in many animal groups. One experiment found that whenever there were three or more mice in a cage, eventually, one would become the scapegoat. The scapegoat would act strange and the other mice would attack it or reject it. The other mice appeared to be quite normal. If the scapegoated mouse was removed from the larger group, eventually another mouse would be scapegoated. When all the scapegoated mice were together all but one (which became the scapegoat in that group) began to act normally.

In scapegoating, family members covertly agree that "we are all okay but this other person sure has problems. If we can't get him or her to straighten out we will have to reject him or her." Scapegoating is a way to deal with the anxiety one feels about one's own sense of self and about being in close relationships. If the focus can be on one who appears to be abnormal, the other family members do not have to look at their own failings.

The scapegoating phenomenon is so common, in fact, that when a problem child develops in a family and all attention is focused on this child, it usually means there are deeper, more basic issues being ignored in the family. Usually, these issues are between Mom and Dad and their anxiety about their relationship with each other. And, of course, their anxieties stem from their experience in their families of origin which they have never looked at or dealt with.

Scapegoating is usually done in such a subtle way that no one, not even the scapegoat, realizes it is happening. It often appears as though the scapegoat is the problem — the disruptive one, the sick one, the unloving one — and the rest of the family is only trying to help the scapegoat.

What makes it even more complicated is that rarely is the scapegoat an innocent victim. Usually the scapegoat, quite unconsciously, volunteers for the role and almost on purpose does things that the family will find upsetting. The scapegoat is usually the person who is most sensitive to the differences between Mother and Father and is the one who most fears their potential separation. Motivated by fears for self's security if they separate, the scapegoat will help Mom and Dad stay together by providing a focus for them outside of their relationship. By helping them to ignore their differences and focus instead on the scapegoat's differences, he or she keeps them together.

QUESTIONS

1. Which child in your family of origin, among your siblings, became most triangled in to the family and took on the role of the problem child?

2. Can you identify what this did for the family (not just how it hindered the family)? For example, what would have happened to the relationship between your parents if there had not been a problem child? Might they have needed to focus on someone else's problem in order to avoid problems between them?

3. Which child might have played this role in your parents' own family of origin?

4. There are various roles that can be assumed by a person in the scapegoat position to draw attention away from other issues in the family. Were any of these roles played in your family: ___ smart aleck ___ clown ___ crazy genius ___ loafer ___ idiot ___ social outcast ___ saint ___ sinner ___ beauty queen (or king)?

5. What were some of the labels that were applied to you as a child? What were the positive labels? The negative labels?

6. What impact did these labels have on your identity and participation in the family?

One triangle that appears in some families is grandparent, parent, grandchild. When a grandparent has little influence over the parent, the grandparent may form a coalition with the grandchild as a way of strengthening his or her position with the parent. In this case, grandparent and grandchild will tend to see each other as friendly equals. If the grandparent does exercise authority over the parent, the motive for a coalition between grandparent and grandchild is missing and it is likely that grandparent and grandchild will not be as close.

Another kind of extended family triangle is mother's brother, son, and husband. This tends to occur in situations where there is a strong authoritarian husband and a wife who has difficulty dealing with him. Her brother might step in to give some warmer, more caring parenting to her son and show the family how to deal with the husband.

The process of differentiation requires that you start detriangling by getting out of the coalitions. Refuse to take sides between two feuding family members. Don't initiate coalitions by looking for support or strength from other members to bolster your position. Take independent positions and deal with others as individuals, based on your own wants and perceptions.

One sign of being involved in a triangle is when you make decisions on the basis of loyalty. If getting closer to one person feels like disloyalty or betrayal to another person, you are involved in a triangle.

Example

Candace wanted to invite to her wedding an aunt and uncle who had been cut off from the rest of the family for many years. Her grandparents told her that they considered her invitation an insult and they wouldn't come if she insisted on inviting the aunt and uncle. After thinking about the risk involved, Candace told her grandparents that she wanted them at the wedding very much but also wanted her aunt and uncle there and was still going to invite them. Her grandparents first claimed she was betraying them and their care for her over the years. Later, they relented and came to the wedding. Surprisingly, the two sides of the family hit it off and have been friendly ever since.

It doesn't always end this well when detriangling. But regardless of what Candace's relatives had chosen to do, she was true to herself and freed herself from an unhealthy coalition.

QUESTIONS

1. Family members often have a sense of being debtors and creditors to each other. Do you personally have a sense of either owing or being owed to with members of your family of origin?

2. What about other members of the family and your parents in their family of origin?

3. What is the impact of these balances of loyalty on the total family? How do they affect relationships in the family?

4. THE WORLD IS A STAGE — ROLES IN THE TRIANGLE

There are three basic roles in triangles and their coalitions. These are persecutor (P), victim (V), and rescuer (R). Not every scene in the dramatic cycle of the triangle has all roles present, but the overall cycle usually contains all of them. Every member of the family can play each role at different times, so that the persecutor may switch roles and become the victim or the rescuer. That, for example, is what happened when Sue's father (P) was angry with Mother (V). Mother, in tears, appeared defenseless to Sue (R), who saw Father as abusive. She came to the rescue of Mother and attacked Father for being dictatorial, thus becoming the persecutor, with him as the new victim. Mother then felt bad about what Sue said to Father and became the new rescuer of Father and persecutor of Daughter. Sue then got angry at her mother and persecuted her, saying she was weak and should stick up for herself more often. Then Father came to the rescue of Mother and persecuted Daughter, the new victim, saying she shouldn't talk to her mother that way.

Though it is still a sign of fusion in the family when members take on these roles, it is healthier when every member can play all the roles equally well. Families tend to become less functional and less able to adapt when particular roles get attached to particular people: when, for example, Dad is always the persecutor, Mom is always the victim, and Daughter is always the rescuer.

Triangle roles are just refinements in the process of controlling the closeness and distance in a relationship. Each of the three roles can represent either over- or under-functioning even though, on the surface, it appears rescuers are over-functioners and victims under-functioners, with persecutors able to be either.

Victims appear to others to be powerless and think of themselves as powerless. In fact, they are usually the most powerful person in the family. They are able to elicit much attention from others and are almost always taken into account when decisions are made. Victims often know full well how to exploit their helpless, pitiful state and arouse a rescuer to action.

The victim is able to get others involved in solving the victim's problems. They don't have to be responsible for themselves if others will do it for them. Many people go to a therapist hoping the therapist will rescue them by telling them what to do or even doing it for them. Family members do the same with their assigned rescuer.

In addition to the personal payoffs victims receive, they help rescuers and persecutors by getting the focus off of them. The rescuers don't have to pay attention to their feelings about themselves and their sense of adequacy when there is a victim around to take care of. Persecutors don't have to be responsible for their own role in the problems at hand if there is a victim around to blame.

Almost always, victims are "willing victims" because by under-functioning they are helping the family in some way. This is true of nearly all family scapegoats they volunteer for the job. By under-functioning they keep the attention on themselves rather than on something else in the family that is upsetting and potentially destructive. If the rescuer stops being responsible for the victim, then the victim may start being responsible for him/herself, assuming no one else is around to start over-functioning for him or her.

The three basic roles in the triangle: persecutor, victim, and rescuer

Like both victims and rescuers, persecutors are also anxious and in-secure people. This is not always obvious since they often portray them-selves as extremely secure and confident, often with righteousness and morality on their side. Indeed, their favorite words are should, ought, must, and have to. Like rescuers, they often take on responsibility for others because they know the correct way to do things, or they at-tack others for doing things inadequately (meaning not doing it the way the persecutor wants it done). Like each of the other positions, perse-cutors believe that others are responsible for the way they are. It is not uncommon for rescuers to become persecutors when the victim refuses the help offered by the rescuer.

QUESTIONS

1. Who are the persecutors, victims, and rescuers in your family of origin?

2. Have you ever not fulfilled your expected role? What was the result?

3. What roles do you think your parents played as children in their families?

Chapter 7

WHO'S ON FIRST? — BIRTH ORDER AND GENDER POSITION IN THE FAMILY OF ORIGIN

by Lois Richardson

I wish I could shimmy like my sister Kate.

— A. J. Piron

Added to all the other ingredients that go into the pot of our personality formation are our birth order and sex. The way we think about ourselves and how we react to and treat others outside the family starts with how our family members relate to us as males or females and as first, last, or middle born.

Freud was the first of the psychotherapists to note that a "child's position in the sequence of brothers and sisters is of very great significance for the course of his later life." It has long been recognized, for instance, that oldest children have certain characteristics in common, such as being achievement-oriented and having leadership qualities. There are also certain common characteristics among those of other birth orders and sex. The younger brother of sisters, for example, grows up in a different environment from the younger brother of brothers and will have some different characteristics. The difference in birth positions accounts to a great extent for the tremendous variety of personalities among the children of the same parents.

The characteristics of the various birth orders summarized in this chapter are based on the research and writings of many authorities in the field and primarily on the work of Walter Toman, an Austrian psychologist. Toman studied thousands of "normal" families and consistently found that people who were in the same birth and gender position had similar characteristics. His book *Family Constellation* (Springer) is a classic in the field and is highly recommended.

Toman's studies have been duplicated by many other researchers with similar results. Others disagree with him in some areas, or, like Lucille K. Forer and Alfred Adler, have used a different approach in studying the concept.

There are an infinite number of combinations and variations of birth order position, depending upon the number of siblings, their gender, and their relative ages. However, all sibling positions are some combination of those listed in the following pages. For example, a middle brother of brothers may have the mixed characteristics of both the older and younger brothers described here. Depending on how many younger and older brothers there are and the total age span, he will be more or less like an oldest or youngest brother.

The situation may be further complicated by a distribution of sexes as well. An oldest brother of brothers and sisters will have the characteristics similar to an oldest brother of brothers and an oldest brother of sisters.

If there are more than five or six years between siblings, each will be more like an only child, though they will also have some of the characteristics of the pure form of the birth and gender order they are closest to. For example, the oldest sister of a brother who is eight years younger will be most like an only child (which she was for eight years), but will have some of the traits of an oldest sister of brothers.

Where there are large age gaps between groups of siblings, sub-groups will form, with those in each sub-group developing the characteristics of the position they occupy within that group. For example, in a family where there are three female children, then a gap of six years followed by two males two years apart, the youngest male will be more like a youngest brother of brothers than like a youngest brother of sisters. The greater the age gap, the more this will be true. The smaller the age difference between siblings, the more influence they have on each other.

These descriptions of the birth and gender order positions do not say what anyone should be like; they merely report what most people are usually like. They are descriptive, not prescriptive. The intent is to help you see the possible origin of some aspects of your personality and give you some understanding of why others in your family act the way they do. It is important to keep an open mind about yourself and be willing to look closely at your own characteristics before dismissing the descriptions of your birth order and sex. The description may not fit, but if it does, it can help you in your process of self-change.

It is particularly helpful to see how the combination of your partner's and your own birth order may have affected your relationship (or how your parents' have affected theirs). Other things being equal, some matches usually work better than others simply because the birth and gender order are well matched. Being well-matched in this case means most nearly duplicating the age and gender arrangement you each were used to as children. For example, the youngest sister of brothers usually does best with an oldest brother of sisters. Both are comfortable with that particular relationship of sex and relative age.

Since many of our basic assumptions about life come from our place in the sibling order, we have the least difficulty in later life when that place is maintained in some form in our adult relationships. If we are in a situation quite different from what we were familiar with as children, we may have more difficulty coping with it. Even if our original situation was less than desirable, it is familiar, and we tend to prefer the devil we know to the devil we don't know, as we are better prepared to deal with that known devil.

The youngest sister and oldest brother combination usually works well not because of any inherent goodness in them, but because it's the most comfortable arrangement for those two people. They know how to act with each other. Even if they have problems with each other, their problems in another match might be greater.

In contrast is the relationship of an oldest sister of sisters married to an oldest brother of brothers. In this case, both are used to being the eldest and therefore the "authority" and neither is used to family peers of the opposite sex. They would likely conflict over control and lack understanding of the other sex.

Although the best match may often be the one that most closely duplicates the family of origin arrangement, it isn't always the one people seek. We are often attracted at first to people who have many things in common with us. Thus, two oldest children may be able to sympathize with each other and share common frustrations and burdens. They may feel they have found a kindred spirit. After living together for a while they find their spirits may be kindred, but their personalities are in constant conflict over who is boss of the household.

For most of us, of course, it is too late to choose a spouse or partner of complementary birth and gender order. We are already stuck with our choice! If it turns out to be one of the poor matches, there is still hope; we simply have to work harder at overcoming that particular handicap. Being aware of this source of trouble in a non-complementary relationship can make the problems more manageable. It is helpful to know something as simple as birth order can account for major differences in a relationship and neither person is necessarily to blame. It is just a matter of differences that are more challenging than most to live with. Once you understand, for instance, that as an oldest brother of brothers and an oldest sister of sisters married to each other you are likely to have conflicts over authority, you can stop blaming each other when those conflicts arise and just accept it as a difficult combination. You may, perhaps, even learn to laugh at your conflicts as you catch yourselves acting just like an oldest sister of sisters or an oldest brother of brothers. Although the research is scanty, it would seem that the birth order position of eldest, youngest, etc., also has an impact in same-sex relationships. That is, two youngest sisters of sisters in a relationship may have more to deal with than an oldest sister of sisters and a youngest sister of sisters do.

This is also true of friends we have as adults. Those we get along well with are likely to be in a complementary birth order position. If they are in a non-complementary position, it may explain any tension that exists in the relationship.

Example

Joan and Arla were neighbors and enjoyed each other's company, shared the same interest in local politics, and had children the same age. However, they often had strong disagreements about a variety of issues, especially the subject of men in general and their spouses in particular. Arla always defended the actions of men, made excuses for her husband's poor treatment of her, and was critical of feminists. Joan thought Arla's husband treated her intolerably and couldn't understand why Arla put up with him. It was no surprise to learn that Arla was the oldest sister of two brothers (and therefore used to taking care of and spoiling men) and Joan was an only child (and most interested in her own and other women's rights).

The relationships between parents and children can also be affected by a complementary or non-complementary birth order. For example, the youngest brother of brothers whose father is the oldest brother of brothers may have a close relationship with his father, while the youngest brother of sisters would probably not get along as well with the same father.

Knowledge of parents' birth orders can be helpful in understanding why they were the kind of parents they were. For example, a youngest sibling rarely has any experience in taking care of others and usually has more difficulty parenting. Often, parents who are the youngest in their own family of origin will expect their own children to assume responsibilities for the family.

Some people think that birth order descriptions tend to sound like horoscopes. However, research does support the descriptions in general. No one fits their birth order description exactly because a number of other family variables modify these characteristics. These variables are explored in greater depth in the follow-up volume to this book *Birth Order and You*, also published by Self-Counsel Press. That book goes into greater depth around the descriptions and gives more examples. Many of the examples are of famous people.

Most readers have exclaimed that these descriptions fit them almost exactly. Others have not recognized themselves at all. It may be useful for these readers to give the descriptions to a partner or a good friend asking if the description fits the reader. Sometimes we are blind to our own characteristics. It is not unusual for a husband, for example, to say, "It got my wife to a T, but it doesn't fit me at all." Then the wife may say the same thing in reverse. Accepting these descriptions as accurate may require a certain amount of personal objectivity. If all others agree that the description does not fit the reader, then further inquiry into the other variables could be explored.

1. THE OLDEST CHILD

To begin with, oldest children are only children at first. Then, just when they have become accustomed to their privileged position with their parents, they are displaced by a new baby. When this displacement comes within five years or less, it is an extreme shock to the oldest child. After five years, the oldest has a place in the world outside the family and a pretty well established identity, so is less threatened by the newcomer.

When the second child is a different sex, the negative reactions of the first child are not as dramatic; there is less direct competition so the oldest child characteristics described here are much less pronounced.

When the second child is the same sex, however, the threat to the first seems much greater. This leads to one of the common patterns of oldest children: They try very hard to be good so their parents will continue to love them rather than their replacement. The parents unknowingly reinforce this by telling the oldest he or she is bigger and smarter than the newborn and therefore superior, even though the newborn now gets most of the parents' attention. The parents also expect the oldest to set a good example for younger siblings — to be a big girl or boy — and to help take care of the baby. As a result, oldest children usually have many parental qualities; they can be nurturing and they are often able to handle responsibility well and assume leadership roles. More than half the presidents of the United States have been oldest male children, and 21 of the first 23 American astronauts were oldest or only children.

This sense of responsibility can also be a burden, and oldest children may turn into perfectionists and worriers, who dare not make mistakes or disappoint their parents or other authority figures. If the standard of achievement in a particular family is measured by success in crime, the oldest will be a high achiever in that, too. The oldest may become the godfather, or like Hitler, a megalomaniacal world leader.

The emphasis on high achievement tends to make oldest children more tense, more serious, more reserved, and less playful than others. They usually work hard and are conscientious at whatever they do, although they find it difficult to accept criticism.

Another early and unique influence on oldest children is the parents' newness at parenting. They are usually very excited about the birth of the first child and they look forward to it eagerly and pay close attention to everything that happens with the baby; the first smile, the first word, and the first step are all exclaimed over and recorded in the baby book. Later-born children are taken more for granted, and each successive child probably receives less attention and praise for these routine accomplishments. But the first child is the grand experiment, and the parents don't really know what they're doing. As one playwright said, "Children ought to be like waffles; you throw away the first one."

The oldest children learn to identify with the parents and often end up as guardians of the status quo, first preserving the family traditions and morality for their younger siblings, then trying to enforce it on the world. They may become so rigid that they are unwilling to accept any change or compromise.

Partly because of using their power to get their own way and partly because they tend to be undemonstrative and too serious, oldest children often find it more difficult than others to make friends. They usually have just one close friend. They tend to be sensitive to personal slights, and show little tolerance for the mistakes of others.

The sex, and number, of younger siblings play a crucial role in the final personality development of the oldest. If all the younger siblings are of the opposite sex, the characteristics just described will be moderated considerably. If the younger ones are all of the same sex, especially if there are two or more, the characteristics will probably be intensified.

1.1 Oldest sister of sisters

The oldest sister of sisters is usually bright, strong, and independent, able to take care of herself and others. She tends to be well-organized and domineering, and may find it difficult to accept advice or help from others. She is outgoing and self-confident, or acts that way, and often has an opinion about everything — the right opinion. She usually tried to please her parents by being good and tidy.

The more sisters she has, the less likely she is to marry happily or marry at all. Her best match is with the youngest brother of sisters, who is used to having a stronger woman in his life. She can take care of him and run his life without too much objection from him. A youngest brother of brothers will also accept her leadership. An only male child is sometimes a good match since he is not used to having peers and will accept her in a mother-like role. The oldest brother of brothers is usually the worst match, because they both want to be in charge, so they are likely to have a constant power struggle. Since neither are used to the opposite sex, they may find it difficult to be very understanding of male/female differences and may be likely to dismiss each other with comments like, "All men (or women) are such and such." When the oldest sister of sisters has children, she often loses interest in her spouse and turns most of her attention to mothering. She is often an overpowering and overprotective mother, but also nurturing. She usually prefers to have girls.

Her closest female friends are likely to be youngest or middle sisters just like at home. She may also have much in common with another oldest sister of sisters and they will get along if they aren't involved in any projects together where there is likely to be a power struggle.

1.2 Oldest sister of brothers

The oldest sister of brothers is usually a strong, independent woman. She is down to earth and sensible, with a healthy ego, although she may at times appear self-effacing.

Men are often the most important thing in the world to her — her most precious possession. The more brothers she has, the more this is likely to be true. She may gladly give up her own work to take care of a spouse, set his goals for him, run his household, and take care of his children.

Men tend to like an oldest sister of brothers because she is a good sport; she doesn't usually compete with them and often reminds them of mother, so much so that they may not think of her romantically. If she had many brothers, it may be harder for her to settle for just one man to marry; she would like to have a lot around. Even if married, she is likely to have other men in her life in some way, and act as patroness for them.

Her best choice for a husband is usually the youngest brother of sisters. It's the arrangement they are both used to. She will lead and nurture him when he wishes. A youngest brother of brothers may accept her leadership, but may have some difficulty with her femaleness.

The oldest brother of brothers is often a poor match for her since they may have many conflicts over who is boss. The arrival of children usually takes away some of the tension, as they will both like having youngsters around again.

The oldest sister of brothers usually wants to have children — they are her second most precious possession (sometimes even the first if they are boys).

Her female friends, if any, are likely to be youngest sisters of sisters or middle sisters. An only female child could be a good friend too.

At work the oldest sister of brothers is usually a congenial, though not hard, worker. She may act as a mediator when there are conflicts, but she doesn't try to take over. She may make subtle suggestions for improvement to a male boss and allow him to take the credit. If she is in a leadership position, she usually handles it with care, being tactful and delegating work well, often because she doesn't think it worth her time.

1.3 Oldest brother of brothers

The oldest brother of brothers is usually the boss. He is often a leader of men, and likes to be in charge in all aspects of his life. He is usually quite meticulous in his person and his possessions. He may be a perfectionist in many ways, from wanting the tidiest of houses to wanting to win every game.

He is usually successful at what he does. He may get along well with others, especially men, but is usually not on intimate terms with anyone. He won't admit it or ask for it, but he likes women to mother him. He expects a lot from a wife, but usually gives little.

He is usually best matched with the youngest sister of brothers, who may be a tomboy, though cute, and who likes men very much. However, for it to work, she must be willing to cater to him more than a youngest sister usually does.

The oldest sister of brothers may be a good match since she will be maternal. Their conflict will probably be over who knows best, though she will try to humor him along. The worst match would be with the oldest sister of sisters; there could be rank and sex conflicts for both of them. They would probably relate like two sovereign monarchs forced to share a castle together.

He is usually a strict, conservative parent, and the children, especially the oldest, may often feel misunderstood by him.

At work he often either accepts the authority of a male superior and emulates him or tries to usurp the superior's position. He is most likely to end up as a lawyer, a minister, an economist, a politician, an astronaut, or the president of a company or of a country.

1.4 Oldest brother of sisters

The oldest brother of sisters is usually much more easygoing and fun-loving than the oldest brother of brothers. He believes life and love are important. He may be in some ways a hedonist, but a considerate, unselfish one.

He is often very fond of women, and is kind and considerate to them. He gets along well with almost all women, though is usually best matched with the youngest sister of brothers, which duplicates exactly the situation he is used to. There could be conflicts over who is the leader if he marries the oldest sister of brothers, but the arrival of children tends to lessen their competition. The youngest sister of sisters may submit to his authority, but be too prissy for his tastes. The oldest sister of sisters is usually the most difficult match, though he could probably handle it since he is good at pleasing all females.

In any match, his wife is usually more important to him than his children, though he is a good father — concerned, but not overly strict.

The oldest brother of sisters is not usually one of the boys, though he is on good terms with most men. The more sisters he has, the more difficult it is to be friends with men — or to settle for just one woman in his life.

At work, this man is usually a good worker, especially if there are women around. He likes to be the leader, but is an easygoing superior who wants the work done, yet not at the expense of enjoying it. He is often happiest in jobs where there are a lot of women around, such as in the theater, the ballet, or the church. He may also be good in public relations and advertising, but his best work, perhaps, is as a pediatrician or an obstetrician/gynecologist.

2. THE YOUNGEST CHILD

Youngest children, like only children, are never displaced by a newborn. They are always the baby of the family, even to the extent that most of them continue to look young or childish even when they are old. Their families also continue to baby them long beyond babyhood.

Because they are the babies of their families, youngest children are special in a way that oldest and middle children are not. They get a lot of attention because everyone else in the family feels some responsibility for taking care of the youngest. They are often indulged more than the other children in the family were, but they are not usually spoiled in a negative way. They just learn to expect good things from life, so usually end up being great optimists.

By the time the youngest child arrives, the parents have had experience in parenting, so they are both less awed by the baby's accomplishments and more relaxed about being parents. They usually are able to just sit back and enjoy this one or, if they are bored with children by this time, ignore him or her. Regardless of their reasons, the parents have fewer expectations of the youngest and put much less pressure on the youngest to achieve. And so, as you might guess, they do achieve less. They also lack self-discipline and often have difficulty making decisions since there was always someone older and wiser around to take care of things for them. They continue to expect others (like a spouse) to solve their problems for them. Or they may go to the opposite extreme of resenting and refusing help.

They tend to have few great ambitions in life and will be the one least likely to follow the family traditions, unless none of their siblings did. If left to their own devices, they often go into the creative arts.

They can be rebellious if they were teased or bossed around too much and may end up working on behalf of other powerless people in society. They are inclined to break social rules and will take potshots at the hierarchy without direct confrontation. They usually have an adventurous approach to life and are open to trying new things.

Because they grew up as the smallest in the family, youngest children learned early that it didn't work to be aggressive to get their way so they developed a manipulative style of getting what they want, either by pouting or by being charming.

They are, in some ways, trying to catch up with their elder siblings for the rest of their lives, but they don't make it unless they go into an entirely different field of work or lifestyle where they can succeed on their own terms.

Even though they may rebel against authority, youngest children are more likely to be followers than leaders and will be eager to please a leader they like. If they happen to be in a leadership position, their followers will like them and their authority will not be taken too seriously. Basically, youngest children remain dependent on others even if they do rebel against the rules. They often choose older spouses and then fight against their control.

Youngest children who have been treated well as children are usually sociable, easygoing, and popular. If they have been unkindly teased as the youngest, they may be shy and irritable with others.

2.1 Youngest sister of sisters

The youngest sister of sisters often acts the youngest all her life. She tends to be spontaneous, cheerful, and adventurous no matter how old she is. She may also be messy, capricious, and some would say bratty at times.

She can be competitive, especially with men, but she is usually flirtatious and plays the feminine role to the hilt. She may try to show up her oldest sister in relationships with men by being more attractive and marrying and having children earlier than her sister.

Her best match in a husband is usually the oldest brother of sisters who will be able to handle her because he sees through her manipulative behavior. The oldest brother of brothers would be an okay match as far as rank but not for gender since neither of them have had any experience of the opposite sex as close peers.

Her poorest choice of husband is usually the youngest brother of brothers. They are likely to have conflicts since neither would nurture the other very well and neither are used to opposite sex peers.

She is not likely to be thrilled about mothering. She usually wants a lot of help with the children, if not from her husband or mother, then from paid help. However, she often has an easygoing style of parenting that children appreciate. Her best friends are likely to be oldest sisters of sisters. The more sisters she has the more she is usually concerned with female friendships and the less with men and marriage, even though she may work hard at attracting men.

At work, she may do well if an older man or woman is able to guide her in using her capabilities. Otherwise, she can be erratic in her work patterns. She is usually the best producer if she is doing some highly skilled, but automatic job, such as a secretary or radio announcer. She is sometimes creative, but often just flighty or unpredictable. She may resent a strong leader, but she is not usually a leader herself and she often has trouble making decisions.

2.2 Youngest sister of brothers

The youngest sister of brothers is usually a congenial, optimistic, attractive, fun-loving woman. She is often the special, favored one in her family, and she usually continues to be favored throughout her life. Things usually just go her way without much effort on her part.

She may be a tomboy and in some circumstances may develop an anger at men and try to compete with them. Usually, however, men are easily tempted by her good looks and compatibility. They tend to flock around her. She, in turn, is often very fond of men. The more brothers she has, the more difficult it may be for her to settle for just one man in her life.

However, she will usually marry happily and consider her husband her prize possession. She may at times be too submissive, though she can also be selfish. She will usually have several male friends or mentors besides her husband.

The best matrimonial match for the youngest sister of brothers is usually an oldest brother of sisters. He tends to be comfortable with women and knows how to cater to a charming one. She is usually pretty secure with men and is the most likely woman to make her best match. She will usually be smart enough to stay away from an oldest brother of brothers, who would be attracted but not overwhelmed by her charms. The youngest brother of brothers is usually the worst match since they may both want to be taken care of and he may not have much patience for their gender differences.

She may want to have children just to please her husband, but she is usually a good mother — so good that her sons may become too attached to her.

Female friends are not usually important to the youngest sister of brothers, and women are often jealous of her.

She is not usually a serious career woman. She often works best as an employee under an older male superior.

2.3 Youngest brother of brothers

The youngest brother of brothers is often like the daring young man on the flying trapeze. He can be headstrong, capricious, and often rebellious. Many assassins are youngest sons (e.g., John Wilkes Booth, Lee Harvey Oswald, Sirhan Sirhan).

He is often unpredictable; he may be in a jolly mood one moment and a foul mood the next. He may excel at something one time, and fail another time. He doesn't usually plan ahead, but lives for the moment and his immediate desires, which makes him flexible most of the time.

He can be carefree and good-natured when things are going well, and he is often a mystic or a romantic. If things are not going well, he usually just leaves; he doesn't like losing. He is used to receiving things and will often squander his money when older.

The youngest brother of brothers is generally gregarious, but usually shy with women. He hasn't had much contact with the opposite sex as a peer and he is often a little afraid of women in addition to not understanding them. He is sometimes too polite, which makes him appear awkward, or he may act the clown around women. The oldest sister of brothers is often the best match for him, particularly if she is the more maternal type. He may let her control his life if she does it unobtrusively. A middle sister with younger brothers is often a good choice as well. The most difficult marriage is usually with a youngest sister of sisters. Neither of them know how to handle the opposite sex and neither of them want to be responsible for running a household or parenting. Having children is usually a strain for him; however, he may be a good companion to his children, especially the boys, since he finds it easy to play at their level.

Male friends are usually more important to him than his wife or children. He often works best when he is competing with another worker or has a superior watching him. He tends to be a follower at work or else he comes up with offbeat, and often unacceptable, suggestions for change. Since the youngest son isn't able to compete intellectually with an older brother while growing up, he often turns to physical activities, such as sports or dance, or creative activities, such as art or acting.

2.4 Youngest brother of sisters

The youngest brother of sisters is usually taken care of by women all his life. In most cases, this is just fine with him. If his sisters were too domineering and bossy with him, he may be rebellious. If he was allowed to be assertive, he usually has high self-esteem and takes it for granted that women like him and will cater to him.

As a child, he may have been doted upon — not only because he was the youngest but because he was unique (being male) and probably desired by the parents. Surveys indicate that most parents want at least one boy and will keep trying until they have one. Because of his special position, he usually does not have to try very hard to distinguish himself. At work, he may be capable, but not always willing to make the effort. If he is excited by it and he is talented, he can become an expert in his field, especially if he has a partner at home taking good care of him. However, he may have difficulty meeting deadlines and staying on the right track. He often works best in areas that have rigid job descriptions and don't require self-motivation.

He may have frequent changes of mood, though he is usually a genial sort. If the family setting has been a good one, he often stays close to his sisters all his life. The more sisters he has, the more difficult it may be for him to settle for just one mate. However, he is usually happy to marry and often has plenty of women to choose from as they are eager to please him even though he may not give much of himself to them. His best match is usually with the oldest sister of brothers, who is good at taking care of men and may be willing to be the woman behind the great man, whether he does anything great or not. No matter whom he marries, his sisters may still try to take care of him.

If he has children, he may consider them an intrusion. A son may be perceived as a rival, so he often does better with daughters. He is usually just as happy with no children, and his wife may have the whole burden of parenting, at least until the children are old enough to share in his interests. If his wife is another youngest, neither of them may want the responsibility of parenting, and they often do best without children.

3. THE MIDDLE CHILD

Middle children, whether the second child of three or one of several in-between children in a family of four or more, are difficult to describe. They are at the same time older siblings to the children who have followed them and younger siblings to those who came before. So, they often end up being having a less distinctive identity. They do not, after all, have a particularly special role in the family the way the oldest child does by virtue of being the first or the way the youngest does by virtue of being the baby. One study of families of three or more children found that the oldest and the youngest were often the favorites in the family.

There are, of course, a huge variety of middle positions, with variations in the ages and sexes and numbers of other siblings — far too many to discuss individually. In general, the middle child will tend to have more of the characteristics of the birth position that he or she is closest to. In other words, a middle child who is close in age to the older sibling or is the second of four or more, will be more like an oldest child. If the middle child is at the lower end of the birth order scale, his or her characteristics will be more like the youngest child. The middle child who is in the exact center will share more of both youngest and oldest characteristics.

Middle children never experience having their parents to themselves and getting as much attention as the first-born. While they benefit from the more relaxed, calmer atmosphere that follows later births in the family, they are soon displaced by the new baby. The middle child then is forced to compete with an older, smarter, stronger sibling and a younger, cuter, more dependent sibling. As a result, the middle child may vacillate between trying to be like the older sibling or like the baby and struggling to create a separate identity. Therefore, middle children as adults tend to be less likely to take the initiative or think independently. In general, they are the lowest achievers academically and the least likely in a family to go to college.

Middle children, since they have neither the rights of the oldest child nor the privileges of the youngest, often feel that life is unfair. One good example of this is an Amazon books reviewer of the first edition of this book. The reader, clearly a middle child, had a strong reaction to the descriptions of this position and gave a one-star rating to the whole book. Every other one of the fourteen reviewers gave the book a four- or five-star rating. One could say that it was possible this middle child felt the "unfairness" of the words describing this position.

Other readers have reacted to how little is said about middles. Because middle children are assumed under younger sibling and older sibling sections in this chapter there is no need to repeat the material here. In a sense, the most extensive descriptions would apply to middle children for this reason.

Middle children lack the authority of the oldest and the spontaneity of the youngest. However, middle children have often learned to be quite adept in dealing with all kinds of people since they have had to learn to live in peace with the very different personalities of their younger and older siblings. They are, therefore, usually friendly to everyone and actively look for friendship. They make good negotiators and are often diplomats, secretaries, barbers, athletes, and waiters — positions that require tact, but not much aggressiveness. Because they also crave attention and affection, they may go into the entertainment field.

The way the sexes and ages of siblings are distributed is most important to the personality development of the middle child. A male with an older brother and younger sister will have different characteristics than a male with an older sister and younger brother.

If all the children are the same sex, the middle child is at the greatest disadvantage. He or she will receive the least attention and have the most need to compete. This middle child will probably be the most uncertain, as he or she will have a nearly equal mixture of characteristics of youngest and oldest, which can lead to feeling anxious and self-critical.

If the middle child has younger and older siblings who are all of the opposite sex, he or she may then receive most of the attention in the family after all. That could result in a middle child who is so pampered that marriage is out of the question since the situation at home is impossible to duplicate. This middle child will also have difficulty making friends with peers of the same sex.

Example:

Rosalie Vestion was the middle girl of five sisters. The first two sisters and the last two sisters were both closer to each other and Rosalie did not feel very connected to any of them. As an adult, unlike her four sisters, she intentionally moved from her hometown in order to stop being referred to as "one of the Vestion girls." In choosing where to move, she looked in the phone books of the major cities she was considering. She chose the city that had "no Vestions in the phone book." This is part of how she worked at creating her separate identity.

* * *

Another middle sister of five sisters was able to carve out a workable position for herself by developing an identity as "the hub sister" around which the others "revolved." As a younger person, she helped feuding sisters to overcome their differences and be more friendly. Over the years, as they each moved to different parts of the world, she kept all the sisters in touch with each other and was always the one to sponsor and organize "sister get-togethers" where they spent a week on a cruise or at a resort.

When there is greater variety in the siblings, it is more difficult to find the appropriate description for the middle child. For example, a female who has an older brother and a younger sister will have a blend of characteristics of a youngest sister of brothers and an older sister of sisters. Depending upon their relative ages, she will probably be more like one than the other, but still tricky to pin down. If there are both older brothers and sisters and younger brothers and sisters, the middle child may be beyond the scope of birth order characteristics. This child will be utterly unique.

4. THE ONLY CHILD

Children who have no siblings have the best and worst of all possible worlds. They are perpetually the oldest and the youngest child in the family. As a result, they have many of the characteristics of an oldest child, yet may remain, in many ways, childish into adulthood.

More than any other sibling position, the only child picks up the characteristics of the same-sex parent's sibling position. For example, a female only child whose mother is the youngest sister of brothers may be more flighty and flirtatious than one whose mother is the oldest sister of sisters. In fact, the only child may be very much like the same-sex parent until faced with some difficulty or stress when the pure only child characteristics will show up.

Since only children are never displaced by younger siblings, they tend to be more at ease with themselves and have a higher self-esteem than oldest children, with less need to control others. They have less resentment of authority and actually expect as well as accept help from others when they need it. Only children generally demand a lot from life. Since parents tend to have the same high expectations for only children as they do for oldest children, only children usually excel at school and at later endeavors. They may even be perfectionists and get very upset if they do not succeed at everything they do. They are, in fact, usually successful; in most tests of scholastic ability they are the highest scorers of all birth positions.

Since only children are not used to living intimately with other children, they often don't know how to cope with intimate peer relationships later in life when they marry or live with someone. They haven't experienced the ups and downs of daily life with others, so they have difficulty accepting or understanding normal mood changes in other people. They don't always realize that the person who is angry with them now may soon be laughing and joking again. They just aren't used to dealing with the complexities of other human beings, and they may, all their lives, be most comfortable when alone. This is not to say that only children don't like other people and even, perhaps, long to be part of a group, but they are accustomed to having mostly their own company. Even same-age childhood friends don't compensate for the lack of actually living with other children.

Having had fewer opportunities for play with other children, only children tend to be less playful than others, and when young, may act like miniature adults. Their early adult conversations give them highly developed verbal skills, but as adults they often end up being the least talkative. The easy give and take of social bantering with peers is not something only children are accustomed to. However, even though it may take them a while to learn to relate easily to any one person, most adult only-children are fairly well-adjusted.

For only children who were born in the 1950s or earlier, there is one other significant factor to consider: Why are they only children? Before the 1960s, it was extremely unusual for parents to have just one child. It is often a sign that there was trouble of some sort with the parents — physical, emotional, or financial — that prevented them from having other children. Today, of course, many people are choosing to have smaller families because of a change in lifestyles. In any case, if there were other problems in the home that kept those earlier families small, those problems would have a significant effect on the only child.

There are, in our culture, differences between male only children and female only children, as discussed below.

4.1 Male only child

In keeping with the findings about the preference of most parents to have at least one boy, male only children are usually more favored than female only children. The male only is often the pet of two adults and, in most families, accustomed to having their continual approval, encouragement, and sympathy. And he thinks the rest of the world should treat him with the same acclaim. When the acclaim comes, however, he tends to take it for granted. Others can't expect much support from him. He usually won't go out of his way for anybody, unless he's just as happy to go that way as another anyway. But it isn't for that reason that the male only child is often a loner. Others may be attracted to him, but he just doesn't pursue friendships and usually prefers his own company.

For a mate, he can take or leave just about any woman. He really isn't well suited to any peer relationship; he's used to having his parents take care of his basic needs while letting him be the little genius. So the partner of a male only child is often expected to make life easier for him without getting much in return.

Since he would be an oldest brother if there had been other children, he is sometimes best matched with a younger or middle sister of brothers. The oldest sister of brothers could do well at being a mother for him. Another only child is usually the most difficult mate for an only child. Both of them may have trouble dealing with the stress and strain of a close peer relationship. Neither of them is used to the opposite sex, and both may want the other to play parent. When only children do marry each other, they often decide (wisely) not to have children.

If the male only child has children, his wife usually has to take the sole responsibility for them; he rarely wants to be involved with parenting.

The male only child, like the oldest, is often a high achiever. In general, he expects his work situation to be set up so that it shows off his achievements, much like his parents' home did.

4.2 Female only child

The female only child often has an underlying sense of herself as a special person — Her Highness — and she is often hurt if others don't treat her that way. She may crave approval, if not adoration, especially from the men in her life. She often has difficulty understanding others unless they are like her. She is at once mature for her years and perpetually childish.

The only girl child is often overprotected by her parents and that can lead her, as an adult, to expect similar protection and care from friends and husband. The husband she chooses (and she usually does the choosing) will have to be a flexible, easygoing, good-natured man, able to cope with her wilfulness. An older man is usually best, someone who is amused rather than threatened by her capriciousness and her tendency to test his love. Like the male only, the female only is not well suited to any particular birth order spouse. The best choice is an oldest brother of sisters or (since she would have been an oldest) the youngest brother of sisters. A middle brother of sisters may work also.

Another only child is the most difficult match, as it is unlikely that he will worship her sufficiently or that she will be able to cater to his needs. They have a better chance if they have strong professional or recreational interests in common. They are the least likely of all couples to choose to have children.

If a female only child has children, her husband will probably have to do most of the parenting, which will be all right if he is the oldest or an older middle of brothers and sisters.

Her female friends are likely to be oldest sisters of sisters or sometimes youngest sisters of sisters. She, more than the male only child, will want to have friends and may seek intimacy without having the skills to attain it easily.

A female only is usually quite intelligent and competent, but her talent may be wasted unless she has the ideal work situation, which is a congenial environment where she can work alone or for a kind, older man.

5. TWINS

If there are no other children in the family, twins will act like two siblings of whatever gender they are, without the age conflict. They will both have some characteristics of the youngest and oldest of their sex. However, in families where the parents emphasize that one was born before the other, particularly if there were several hours between the births, the older one may take the role of the oldest and treat the younger like a younger sibling. All twins are unusually close to each other and if they are the same sex, they often act as one person.

When there are other children in the family, the twins will both have more of the characteristics of the birth position they share. For example, if twin boys are the youngest in a family of girls, they will be a lot like a single youngest brother of sisters.

Twins score the lowest of all birth positions in intelligence tests, probably because their greatest influence is on each other and they are at every stage of life equally knowledgeable. They are also less willing than others to pay attention to and learn from elders, whether siblings, parents, or teachers. They are too much their own little team. In fact, other siblings or classmates may have little to do with them. And it may even be difficult for them to leave each other to marry. Even male/female twins have trouble separating, though they are at least used to a close peer of the opposite sex. Identical twins are the most difficult to separate. They often marry twins. Sometimes, they may share one lover or friend without conflict because they think of themselves as one person.

QUESTIONS

1. What do the birth orders of your parents explain about their ways of parenting?

2. Do you see ways that your birth order has had an impact on your intimate relationships or how you function in your job?

3. If you have children, do you see differences in them that might be ascribed to their sex and birth order?

Note: For more detailed information about the theories of birth order and the characteristics of all birth order positions and sexes, see *Birth Order & You*, by Ronald W. Richardson and Lois A. Richardson (Self-Counsel Press).

Chapter
8

DOING THE WORK

If you cannot get rid of the family skeleton, you may as well make it dance.

— George Bernard Shaw

Sue was able to make the changes in her life and her experiences with her family when she went to a therapist who introduced her to family of origin work. She learned that it was work for her and that her therapist had no easy answers. He showed her how to do the basic steps outlined in this chapter, and she did the work.

In the process of doing this she set some personal goals for how she was going to be different and how she would deal with pressure from her family to stay the same.

This chapter explains the steps that Sue and others have followed in doing family of origin work. This is where the book has been heading — the point of it all. And this is where the work begins for you also.

The reactive patterns developed throughout life are so deeply ingrained they are almost "natural," in the sense of being a part of human nature. They are not easy to change or control. In addition, your own uniquely developed stances toward togetherness and separateness, and your level of anxiety, are deeply ingrained. They are part of your basic character. You will not be doing yourself a service if you think, "I should be able to do this better," or "I'm useless at doing this work because I get so easily triggered into reactiveness," or something along these lines.

Do this work at your own pace and keep your expectations realistic. If you move in slow, easy, and manageable steps, you will get to where you want to go. A good way to frustrate yourself, however, is to expect too much personal change too soon.

Keep the goal of this work before you in clear focus. It is meant to change you, not others. You are not doing this work either "for" your family or "to" your family. This work is not just a more sophisticated psychological tool for getting them, or getting back at them, or getting even, or showing them, or blaming them.

Remember, you developed your character. Your family provided an environment and their own personality styles, and they are responsible only for that. They are not responsible for what you did with that. You reacted to that environment and those personality styles in your own unique way (as did your brothers and sisters if you have them). No one made you the way you are; the good news about this is that it means you can change you. Your changing does not depend on other people changing. You no longer have to react automatically, as you did in your childhood, to the context or environment or style they created. You can be your own person. To do that you must take responsibility for yourself and stop blaming others.

To get started, read this chapter through once to see what is involved; then go back to step one and proceed to do the work. There are seven steps to work through; each one has at least one specific task to complete before you move on to the next step. None of these steps can be completed quickly; this project takes time and commitment. You may also find that you have to go over some steps a number of times to reassess your work, and allow family members to adjust to your changes.

STEP 1 — THE BEGATS: WHO IS IN YOUR FAMILY?

The first step involves clarifying exactly who is in your family. This is not always known or easy to find out. Parts of families get lost when a member is cut off or moves away and doesn't communicate with the rest of the family. It is essential to know what caused those family members to drop contact, move away, or whatever, because they had an impact on those who had an impact on you even if you never knew or met them. For example, an alcoholic grandfather may have been the motivation for a teetotaling parent, which affected your attitude toward drinking.

Even though you can't see these lost family members, they are hanging there in your family mobile and affecting its movement and balance.

Example

Naseem had had a difficult time with his father from the time he was eight or nine years old, all through his teens. His interests did not fit those of what the father thought they should be, that of a masculine teenage boy interested in sports, cars, and so forth. Naseem's interests were what his father considered feminine. The father was extremely critical of him and Naseem suffered from this. He made attempts to fulfill his father's wishes but just never felt he was able to, as well as not being very interested in them. When he was 25, Naseem told his parents that he was homosexual. His father was outraged and refused to have anything to do with him. When doing his family of origin work later, Naseem discovered that he had an uncle he had never known of, his father's younger brother, who was homosexual. His father detested his brother. Naseem then understood much more clearly the source and context of his father's feelings.

So first you have to develop a picture of who is in the family. The best way to do this is to draw a genogram. Examples of genograms have been used in previous chapters. A genogram is a graphic portrayal of the members of a family. It is a good way to get a picture of who is in a family and of the history of relationships in that family.

A genogram should include the names and ages of all family members. It should give dates of birth and death and dates of marriages, separations, and divorces. It should cover a minimum of three generations from yourself back to the generations of your parents and grandparents.

The common symbols and an example of a three-generation family are given on the next two pages.

Here is a narrative of what this three-generation genogram tells you. Jim Lee was born in 1915. Ivy Hill was born three years later in 1918. In 1932 she married Jim and they had four children born to them with one miscarriage. Bill, the first child, died after living only a year. Then the twin girls were born in 1936. The miscarriage was in 1938 and then Dave was born in 1939. Their marriage ended when Ivy died in 1979.

Jerry Abbott, who was born in 1935, married Sue Lee in 1954. In 1957 they adopted Bill into their family. Bill was born in 1955. Two years after the adoption, Dick was born. At the age of 21, in 1980, Dick began living with Gail Hope who is two years older.

In 1960 Ann Lee married John Stevens who was born in 1930. Five years later they had their only child, Lois.

A GENOGRAM

Basic symbols

☐ 1915	— male (square), with birth date
○ 1918	— female (circle), with birth date
⊠ 1933-34	— dead male, with dates of birth and death
○—○ 1936	— twin girls
✕ 1938	— miscarriage or abortion
☐ 1915- —1932— ○	— marriage with dates (husband goes at left side, wife on right)
⊠ ○—○ ✕ ☐ 1933-34 1936 1938 1939	— father, mother, and children in order of birth from left to right

Other common symbols

NITE ☐ ---- WOLF ○ 1950-55	— common-law or living together with dates, with family names above
☐ 1957 ⁄ 1959-60 ○	— separation, with dates when separation began and when couple reunited, as well as date when married
☐ 1950-62 ⁄⁄ ○☐	— divorce with dates of marriage, children are with mother after divorce
☐ 1957⋮ ○ 1955-	— foster or adopted child with birth date below and date of entering family above

(The last name goes above the circle or square and the first name inside.)

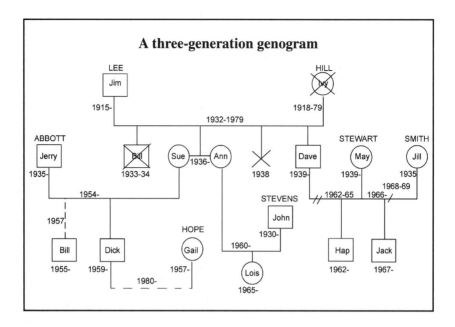

A three-generation genogram

In 1962 Dave Lee married May Stewart who was also born in 1939. That marriage ended in divorce after three years and their only child Hap is living with his mother May. One year after the divorce Dave married Jill Smith who was born four years before him. They had a son, Jack, and a year later they had a brief separation. During the separation Jack continued to live with Dave.

As you can see, a lot of information is succinctly contained within a genogram. Many people comment that, once they have drawn their own three-generation genogram, they have a whole new sense of their family. For the first time, they see their family as a whole and are able to see patterns and relationships they've never noticed before.

Try the following exercise to get a better sense of your place in your family of origin.

DRAWING YOUR OWN GENOGRAM

Draw your own three (or more) generation genogram. Include as many people, names, and dates as you know. Don't worry about not having all of them.

It may help, after a few tries on smaller sheets of paper, to draw the genogram on a large piece of newsprint or butcher paper. Some people even use larger sheets. You may want to use different colors to make distinctions between generations or blood lines. Feel free to do this in any way that helps you see your family more clearly.

If you have any good friends (not family) who would be willing to listen, present your genogram to them and tell them what you know about each family member and the character of the relationships. Encourage them to ask you questions about the family.

STEP 2 — HELLO, MOM. REMEMBER ME?: CONTACTING FAMILY MEMBERS

Once you have developed your family genogram, make copies of it and send or give it to members of your family. Ask them if it is correct, as far as they know, and if they can add the names, or dates, or persons that you don't have on it. This usually makes for an excellent beginning in doing family of origin work and it helps to prepare for visits and discussion later on.

Along with the copy of the genogram you could say something like, "I'm trying to understand myself better and you could really help me do this by giving me whatever information you have about our family." Since the book and TV movie *Roots*, people are quite familiar with this kind of approach and understand it. Doing the family tree is a popular activity.

Some people are hesitant to ask for this information from their relatives. They fear the relatives will react negatively, but the evidence shows that this fear is rarely confirmed. If you make it clear that the family members can be a help to you, and that their help is appreciated, people usually are eager to share much of what they know about the family. They may even get excited about it themselves and start working on it with a lot of energy.

Example

Noah's parents divorced when he was less than a year old and he grew up with just his mother. Through the first 35 years of his life he never talked with her or asked her any questions about his father. She, likewise, never volunteered any information about his father. Noah took this to mean that she would be uncomfortable talking about him and so he never asked. Noah had a lot of theories about why she was uncomfortable about it and had, for a long time, believed that he was conceived out of wedlock. When he began to do his family of origin work, he wrote to her and finally asked her to tell him about his father and what had happened between them. He was quite afraid of her reaction since he thought he was breaking a family rule. He received a three-page, single-spaced letter that told him the whole story. The letter began with a sense of relief, a "whew, I thought you would never ask!" The mother was quite happy and eager to talk about Noah's father. She had always assumed he would be too uncomfortable to talk about it! He found out many things he had never known, including the fact that his parents had been married five years before he was born.

Time after time, people who start this work think their families will be suspicious or put off by their letter with a genogram attached. And time after time they are surprised by the excited and interested response they receive. People are generally very interested in their family and in sharing their family experience. If they know they are not going to be attacked and that what they have to say will be helpful to someone else, they respond eagerly. Many are just waiting to be asked. They want to share.

Letters and copies of the genogram should be sent to every family member, even your own brothers and sisters. You might think that they won't have any information that you don't have. Don't count on that. They were born into a different family than you were — a family at a different stage of development. Each member will have had different experiences in the family and different perceptions about shared experiences.

Some people think they can't do this work because their parents are dead. In fact, it is likely that there are still people around who knew your parents when they were younger and may even have been close to them. You may find family friends, neighbors, pastors and priests, babysitters and housekeepers, coworkers, and many others who have information they could share about the dead parents.

Examples

Donna's mother was dead. Donna was asked who her mother had talked to when she was alive and had a problem. Donna remembered a close friend of the mother. She contacted her, spent a weekend with her, and got information about her mother that no one else could have given her.

* * *

Another woman lost her parents when she was 12 years old. She vaguely remembered some people who took care of her for a short while after her parents' death. She got in touch with them, and it turned out they had been close friends with her parents and had a great deal to share.

There is one important caution in doing this work. Whenever someone is telling you what another person thought, felt, or did, or about their basic motivations, always treat it as hearsay. It may or may not be accurate. That information is always taken in and shared through the filter of the speaker's own biases and interpretations. Always treat the information as "so and so said," not "this is the way it was."

Always be sure to contact the family members who are supposed to be "crazy," whether they are institutionalized or not. They will have a helpful perspective to offer on family life and history.

Example

A cut-off member of Boris's family had been labelled "crazy" and "eccentric" by the rest of the family and he was told "she's not worth talking to. She just talks gibberish. Leave her alone." He contacted her anyway and found that she was quite sane, though indeed eccentric. She saw family history and related issues much differently from the rest of the family (this is what led to the cutoff) and helped him better understand some puzzling family issues.

There is no particular magic and nothing will necessarily change in the family by looking at family names, dates, and histories. This step will do three things for you, however. First, you will discover and clarify just exactly who is family for you. Second, you will begin to fill in the gaps of information about people and events that have had an impact on you and other family members without your awareness. Third, and most important, you will begin to interact with other family members in a more neutral, less reactive way. It provides a positive way to interact with family and gets them involved in the work. You go to them for their help, for their knowledge and information, and this usually creates warm and positive feelings in others. They like being asked about their experiences.

A goal for your genealogy work is to develop information about every member in every nuclear family in your extended family. Try to find out who did well and who did poorly, what impact members had on each other, and the nature of the relationships in each of these families. This part of the work will extend over many years. Your major focus will be on your own immediate three-generation family, but that work will be augmented over the years as you broaden your awareness of your total family system. The following exercise will help.

CONTACTING FAMILY MEMBERS

Write letters to family members (with attached genograms) as suggested above. Before sending the letters, reread them carefully, or better yet, ask a good friend to read them to be sure that there are no disguised attacks in them and that they represent a genuine, straightforward request for help. See the example of a letter and questions in the Appendix.

Who are you leaving out or avoiding writing to? What is your concern about that person? Might your avoidance be a part of some triangular pattern in the family (e.g., Mother will be upset if you contact the sister-in-law she dislikes)?

STEP 3 — DEVELOPING A HISTORY

Dates and the times of particular events are important, so the next step is to develop a chronological history of the family covering the three generations. A file card system may work best since you can add cards as you develop new information. The card should give the exact date, the event, and your estimate of the impact of the event on the family system.

Getting correct dates is important. One of the mysteries of family life is the variety of dates people will give for a specific event. They will give dates as much as five or ten years wrong and thus obscure significant connections. Time seems to be a very subjective experience when it comes to family history; different members make their own connections. You need to push for accuracy in dating events.

Dates and events important to list include the following: births, deaths, marriages, separations, divorces, major illnesses and hospitalizations, adoptions, job changes, firings and resignations, changes in economic situation, geographical moves, graduations, people moving out of or away from home or back home. In sum, any kind of change in the number, location, and status of family members is significant. As pointed out in Chapter 2, each change of this sort affects the quality of life in the family.

In addition to family dates, you could include on the cards notations of major world or regional events that coincide with family history. For example, the depression of a grandparent might coincide with the Crash of '29 or the disappearance of an uncle might relate to the outbreak of World War II.

You might also want to be clear about what kinds of jobs and work people do. For instance, exactly what was your paternal grandfather's job and what did it involve? How much time was spent away from the family? What was the impact of his job on the family? On your father?

What events led up to the cutoff of one or more family members? How do different people in the family see it? Who is never mentioned or is treated as though they don't exist in the family? What caused this situation? What has been the impact?

These are examples of the kinds of questions that doing a chronological history can help you answer; they will assist you in clarifying the impact of events on your family. They will also help you be clearer about what was going on at the time of your birth and what impact your birth had on the lives of the people in your family.

DEVELOPING YOUR FAMILY HISTORY

Using file cards, chronologically list the major events in the history of your family. Beside the dates, list any major world events that coincide with your family events. Also note the impact that any particular event had on your family.

Show the cards to as many family members as you can. Can you account for any discrepancies in the dates that different family members assign to different events?

How do different family members evaluate the impact of major events on your family?

STEP 4 — DR. LIVINGSTON, I PRESUME?: RESEARCHING

Step 4 is where you begin to pull all the information together and attempt to make some sense of it. In addition to gathering data at this stage, you can begin to identify patterns and develop hypotheses about the operation of your family. These hypotheses will be tested and clarified during your family visits in step 5.

Doing good research is essential to this step. The image of the professional researcher is the best model for you to base your work on. The professional researcher does not have a stake in a certain outcome. The researcher is unbiased, unprejudiced, and interested in all sources and sorts of data. Researchers are curious and ask a lot of questions.

As you work on this step, keep a notebook for the questions you want to ask and pursue. Write down everything that helps you develop a clearer picture of your family and your place in it. It will help if you view your family as a valuable, treasured resource. This means that every family member, even those you feel alienated from, can help. Each holds some pieces to the puzzle. Each has something to offer, or a way to help you, as you go about your work.

This attitude may be difficult for you to adopt, especially with those family members who seem useless, bad, or under-functioning to you. But they may know things about the family you're not aware of and may have skills that you don't share. Avoid thinking about their inadequacies; consider what they have to offer you.

A good place to begin identifying patterns is by looking at the major triangles in the family. First, take a copy of your genogram and use one or more colored felt tip pens to draw the connections between members of the major triangles, or between groups of people in the various corners of triangles. This gives you a sense of your own intuitive feel for triangles in the family.

The next approach to triangles is more methodical. Pick one individual and go through the whole family by imagining this individual in a one-to-one relationship with every other person in the family.

Ask yourself these questions to clarify the relationships.

- What are these two people like when they are with each other? (This is, of course, often difficult to imagine and would have to be checked out in the family visits.)

- How open are they to each other; how anxious are they?

- What kind of automatic reactions do they have with each other?

Do your research

For example, you might try to discover how Mom is like your grandmother, and vice versa. Then relate Mom to every other family member and see in what ways, if any, she is different — where she is more or less anxious, and how she actually behaves in relation to that person.

Go back through the same process with each person and add a third person. For example, what happens to the relationship between Mom and Grandmother when Dad is present?

- What and who changes when you add a third person?

- What new behaviors emerge?

- Who is closest to whom in the threesome?

- How is the closeness and distance handled?

- What impact does the behavior of this triangle have on other triangles and members of the family?

- What happens in the family when this triangle is calm and peaceful? When it is turbulent and highly anxious?

Also look at the triangular roles of persecutor, victim, and rescuer.

- Are they constantly played by the same people or do they shift around with each person playing different roles at times?

- Does one person always play the same role in every relationship?

- What coalitions remain constant?

- What keeps these triangles operative?

- What experiences, situations, and circumstances activate them?

In this part of the work, attempt to focus especially on the relationships before you were born. How did the family get to be the way it was at the time of your birth?

Of course, most of this is pure guesswork, but some of it will have been shared with you previously by family members. It will help highlight the areas you need to focus on in your visits. Write down questions in your notebook.

Then shift your focus to your experience in the family in the various dyadic and triangular relationships. Put yourself in one-to-one relationships with each family member and experience what that relationship is like for you. Then add a third member and examine what happens to your relationship when you use the questions above.

What are the close/distant positions like for you in the triangles?

- Do you want to move closer, or be more distant, or stay where you are?

- What is your anxiety about? Do you fear more the loss of self or the loss of dependency with these persons?

- What physical and emotional experiences do you have in these relationships? How do you interpret the relationships?

- What is going on? How do you deal with it?

- What set steps are there in the triangular patterns? For example, does A get close to B with C on the outside, and then B moves to C with A outside, and then C moves to A with B outside? Or does B continually go back and forth between A and C? Or is A in the outside relation to B when C is present but gets close when C leaves?

- What are the patterns?

- What are the relationships like and how do they change in times of low and high anxiety?

Take another copy of your genogram and draw what you now believe to be the most important triangles. How does this compare with your first drawing? Establish a hierarchy of the five most important triangles in the family, ranking them from one to five in order of importance. See if you can find any patterns of interrelationship between them, or how one will activate another.

Next, look at the chronology of the family that you developed in step 3 and pick out significant events; see if you can determine what impact they had on the family system. What changes occurred in the triangle system when there was a loss or an addition to the family? For example, deaths often create a ripple effect (sometimes waves) in the family. The loss of a significant person in the system requires a whole new set of relationships to emerge and can create new triangular patterns. Some research indicates, for instance, that children who eventually become schizophrenic were born within one year or two after the death of a significant grandparent. They take on a specialness that is an indication of the significance of the death. Another common reaction to a death is for a dependent family member to worry, "What's going to happen to me now that this important person is gone?" In that case, someone else is usually found to replace the dead person, or at least an attempt is made.

Example

Alexandra's father died. She was not able to grieve easily because she was concerned that her mother, who had been very dependent on her dad, would now turn to her to depend on. Rather than being free to focus on her own feelings of loss, Alexandra spent most of the week after his death distancing from and being cool toward Mother and other family members so that they wouldn't get the idea that Alexandra would replace Dad. A brother, who was dealing with the same fears, attempted to designate Alexandra as the appropriate person to look after Mother. So she was also angry at her brother for this pressure and felt guilty about her presumed selfishness.

Other families create new triangles around wills and money at the time of a death. These old, unresolved issues make their presence felt anew. It is not unusual for cutoffs from the family to occur at the time of a death as a way of trying to escape the new triangles.

Go over your chronology and develop some theories about the impact of those events on the family, and when you begin to make your family visits, you can check out the accuracy of your theories. Likely they will change as you get more information, but having the theory will help you focus on the kind of information you want and will be an aid in eliciting the information.

Also, review things like triangular roles, sibling positions and characteristics, the family rules, and the under-functioning/over-functioning patterns. In the case of the latter, when there is, for example, a strongly over-functioning parent, you will probably see at least one child in the next generation who will under-function just as strongly. Then when that person becomes a parent there will probably be at least one child who will over-function for that parent. Sometimes the over/under-functioning will be contained entirely within the marital relationship and the children will be relatively free of the process, but generally over-functioners beget under-functioners who beget over-functioners, and so on. Mixed in with these are the four reactive patterns of compliance, rebellion, criticalness, and cutting off. Attempt to identify who used what ways of coping with their own lack of differentiation and dependency.

Begin to think about the impact your changes in attitude and behavior will have on the family and how they will likely respond.

Example

As a child, Darlene had always over-functioned with her under-functioning mother. When she got married and had children, she continued to be the household servant and catered to the kids, who became under-functioners. As she worked on her family of origin, Darlene was able to predict that there would be some pretty serious shock waves from husband and kids as she stopped being the over-functioner. She saw as well that not only would she have to find a way to deal with their reaction, but she would also have to deal with her own anxiety about their reaction.

RESEARCHING

As you think through each of the issues listed above, keep a notebook just for questions that you want to ask specific people.

Discuss your findings, hypotheses, and questions with an objective friend. Ask for help in thinking of other questions to ask.

STEP 5 — YOU CAN GO HOME AGAIN: MAKING FAMILY VISITS

This step involves going back home to gather information, asking questions you've developed from the previous steps, observing how your family operates, and becoming more aware of your part in the family. There is no point in going home without proper preparation. If you try to skip ahead to this step, your efforts are likely to be frustrated. There are certain "rules" for this type of work that you should try to follow in order to most efficiently and effectively work toward your goal.

First, prepare the individuals you are going to visit before you land on their doorstep. This can be done by letter or phone call, and is best if addressed to individuals. For example, you should send a separate letter to Father and to Mother. Of course, they will be surprised if you've never done this before, but it will help establish the expectation that you want to relate to and spend time alone with each individual.

Second, your visits should be short. Two to four days is an ideal length of time. If you stay longer than that, you may fall into old patterns, become reactive, and lose the objectivity you are striving to maintain. However, because your visits will be short, and because face-to-face meetings with your family members are an invaluable part of the process, it is wise to try to make three to six visits a year. Of course, this will depend on how far away you live and other related circumstances. Times of crisis (illness, death, divorce) or times of celebration (weddings, baptisms, anniversaries, Christmas) are good times to visit. Relationships can be quite flexible, or volatile, and more open during these times.

Third, try to make these visits without your spouse. You may want your spouse to come for support or help, but spouses have their own responses to your family and your place in it, and they usually end up becoming part of one of the triangles. This does not mean they can't participate in normal extended family activities, but they should not be involved with your family of origin work. If your spouse or partner is going to accompany you on a visit, agree ahead of time that he or she will not interfere with, comment on, or help with the process. And don't pull your spouse in by using him or her to excuse your own actions. For example, one man told his parents that his wife didn't want to visit them at Christmas because she preferred being in her own house. It was true, but this man used his wife's preference to hide his own reluctance to spend Christmas with his parents. Basically, he put his wife and his family at odds with each other.

Fourth, try to visit the town or city where you grew up. If your parents no longer live there, try to arrange a visit with one of them back to the old home town. Visiting former homes or significant places will evoke a lot of information and sharing. If your parents grew up in another town, try to visit that one as well. This should be done with each parent separately.

Home sweet home

As you approach your visits, be clear in your mind exactly what you want. What are your questions specifically; or what do you better want to understand? Identify what kind of problems might arise in trying to get the information, and develop some strategies for coping with these problems.

This element of wanting something from your visit is what makes these trips different from duty visits where you are just putting in an appearance. People commonly find that their trips home to do this work become genuinely enjoyable experiences and they often have warmer feelings about their families because of this.

One of the things you will be doing throughout the visit as you gather information, is checking the accuracy of the information you already have and the validity of the hypothesis you have developed about the family system and your part in it. You will find out new things about family members and family relationships, which should affect your theories about the family.

For example, as you ask your mother about her relationship with her mother, or her sister, you will probably get information that will help you understand your mother's behavior toward you in a different light.

The most basic rule in your family visits is never to challenge or condemn family members for what they share or say. Try to remember that their perception of family life is going to be different from your perception. As mentioned before, you need to have the attitude of an objective researcher who is interested in discovering the family members' perceptions. Even if you think the person is deliberately lying, don't challenge or confront this. For whatever reasons, someone may feel the need to lie about an issue and that in itself is significant and of interest.

Rather than debating, you can say something like, "Isn't it interesting that you see it that way? I (or another family member) said or saw it this way. How do you account for that difference in perception?" Even this statement could be harmful if you don't watch the tone of your voice. If there is any sense of accusation on your part, the other person will either close up or get defensive, and you will lose the person as a resource. If your tone of voice reflects a genuine interest in how someone accounts for the discrepancy, you may discover some very interesting information.

Some other things to keep in mind when you are researching and asking questions are discussed here.

(a) Ask as many questions as you have time for. The more questions the better. For every answer you get, think of five more questions to ask. You should never run out of questions. Remember, a researcher is always ready to learn more.

(b) It is essential that you not become emotionally reactive, defensive, attacking, or in any way step out of the researcher role. As long as you keep thinking of questions to ask that reflect your interest in others' perceptions of things, you're on the right track. If you run out of questions, it probably means that you're caught in your own reactions and want to challenge, evaluate, or express your own point of view. If this happens, change the subject or stop for the time being.

(c) Make sure the questions you ask are "real" questions. Real questions ask for information. "What time is it?" is usually a real request for information. "Don't you think it is time we go?"

is not. It is a disguised statement meaning, "I think it is time to go." Don't ask this kind of leading question that seeks to bring a person around to your point of view. A good researcher is genuinely interested in how others think and see things, not in having a personal point of view confirmed. Struggling with this style can be one of the most difficult things you will do in these early visits.

(d) Try to avoid questions that begin with "why." They tend to get defensive responses and rationalizations. "Why did you think that?" will tend to get a justified response, whereas the question "What did you think about that?" will get a more direct and open response.

(e) Confirm your interpretations by using "checking out" questions. For example, a question like, "So what you're saying is that you thought mom always liked me best?" is a way to check out with the other person whether what you thought was meant is actually what he or she did mean. Checking out questions can also start with "Do you mean ..." You take whatever conclusion you drew and play it back with "do you mean ..." in front of it. If your older sister says to you, "I always thought you were a little brat," you can ask, "Do you mean because I would not leave you and your date alone, I was a brat?" She could say, "Well, yes, that too. But that wasn't what I was thinking of. It seemed to me that you always tried to get me in trouble with the folks and would tell on me a lot." If you had assumed you knew what she meant by you being "a brat," you wouldn't have found out what really bothered her.

Always keep in mind that you are seeking this information for yourself. Family members are helping you understand yourself by sharing their picture of what your family was and is like, and their experience in the family. You will find yourself seeing things from a new and enlarged point of view, and perhaps even re-evaluating perceptions of your own.

As mentioned, it is important to visit alone with each member of the family. It is pretty common for family members to sit around in a group and talk about "the old days," which is fun, but a lot of self-censoring takes place in those sessions. People are not always as open at such times. Sometimes it is hard to split up particular family members, like Mom and Dad, but it is appropriate for you to say that you would like to have some time alone with each of them and that you don't always want to be a threesome. Invite each one out separately, for lunch, or a walk, or a drive, for example.

If it is hard for you to ask for that alone time with just one family member, that is interesting information in itself. What do you think makes it hard? How would it be perceived if you made such a request? What happens to you when you think others might have that perception?

Example

Miriam's relationship with her father had always been through Mom. As far back as she could remember she had never done anything with just Dad; Mom had always been along and had done most of the talking. While she was growing up, she heard Mom talk about Dad ("Your dad says this, your Dad thinks that"), but she rarely got a message straight from Dad. Finally she got up the courage (she didn't know what she was afraid of) to invite just Dad out to dinner and a movie with her, alone, without Mom. He gladly accepted, and it was the beginning of a new relationship for them. Then she found out what she was scared of: Mom became quite anxious and wanted to know what was going on and "Why are you shutting me out?" She found out that Mom had always feared being left out of relationships and that had to do with her own sense of value and worth. Miriam saw that even as a little girl she had sensed Mom's anxiety about this and had respected the emotional rule of "don't you and Dad do anything together and leave me out; I will feel bad."

When you are alone with this one other family member, try not to spend your time gossiping about those who are not there. Gossip creates a triangle. That is going to happen, inevitably, but always try to bring the discussion back to an exploration of how the person you're with saw things and felt about things. Don't spend time speculating about the motives and intentions of absent family members.

If the person you are with keeps talking about others, you can keep asking, "And how did that affect you?" or "What did that mean to you?" or "What did you think about that?" Your interest is in what meaning others assign to an event. Rarely does a member of the family let others in on what is going on inside by saying, "When you said that, I thought you meant … and so I felt … and I decided I wanted to … and that's why I did what I did." This is what you are trying to uncover now. You're trying to find out more about how your family members have made sense of their life in the family (not just what they think about a topic; you already know most of that) and what their internal experience has been in relation to each other.

When someone you are talking with begins to get uneasy about what is being said, a general rule is to move the discussion to a focus on the generations above. For example, if you are talking with your mom about your relationship with her, and you begin to sense she is uneasy, begin asking her about her relationship to her mom. If she begins to get uneasy there, ask about her mom's relationship to her mom. What did her mom tell her about that relationship or what did she observe? It may be possible then to come back to the former topic with more ease and perhaps even to your relationship with her (the present generation). Generally, be ready to move back and forth between the generations when the talk becomes too difficult. The biggest problem talking to relatives may well be your own uneasiness and anxiety rather than theirs.

Examples

Ned, who had never spent much one-to-one time with his mother, finally arranged it so they would spend a whole day together on a car trip. He had always said that his mother was hesitant to talk with him and that she would be uneasy in that situation. When he found himself alone in the car with her for the day, he discovered he was the anxious one. Even though he had a lot of questions and things he wanted to know about, he didn't raise any of his questions the whole day. Finally, with only about an hour left of their time together, his mother said, "I thought you said there were some things you wanted to talk with me about." He had an hour of one of the best talks he'd ever had with her, but he missed the possibility of doing more for that visit.

* * *

Callie had avoided talking with her mom about some things between them because she thought her mom would cry and that would be very upsetting to her mother. She'd always thought her mother was uncomfortable with tears in her presence. But she went ahead and plunged into the topic and, indeed, her mother did cry. Then she discovered that she was the one who was uncomfortable with her mom's tears and she was the one who had always avoided the topic.

As you meet with various members of the family, try to tune in to previous perceptions you have had of them. Clarify to what extent those perceptions have been based on direct contacts with the relative, and to what extent they are based on things others have told you about the relative. Often, one's impressions are shaped before actually meeting a relative by the prejudices and stereotypes of other family members. Usually these are put forward in either saint or sinner categories. For example, if your mom believes, and has communicated to you, that your uncle is a "lush," how has that affected your picture of your uncle? How has it affected how you deal with and relate to that uncle?

Finally, throughout the visits, you should be observing yourself and how you tend to function in your family system. Both during and after a visit, check the accuracy of your hypotheses about the family and make any corrections you need to make.

STEP 6 — THIS IS ME, LIKE IT OR NOT: DIFFERENTIATING

After doing your research work and clarifying your own role in the family, you will be ready to identify how you would like to change your functioning. There may be several things you would like changed and you can rank them in order of importance and/or difficulty. Take on the easier changes at first; don't set yourself up for a big failure that will reinforce negative and powerless feelings you may have.

Remember that the focus is to be on changing yourself and your ability to deal with how the family responds when you do make that change. If your goal involves in any way making others change, you will be defeated. You must assume that the way they are is the way they are always going to be. In fact, this will probably not prove to be true. If you are successful in changing your role in the family, there will likely be changes in the family as well. If you stay true to yourself, stay close to the family members, and don't react to their attempts to get you to be the way you were, they will, most likely, adapt to your new behavior, and all the relationships will be different.

This means that your goals shouldn't be greater family closeness, warmth, or similar things that we often wish for our families. These things may happen as a result of your family visits, but they won't happen if they are your goal.

For you to become a well-differentiated, emotionally mature person, you have to think from an "I" position rather than a "you" or "we" position. Having an "I" position means that you —

- define and clearly state your own beliefs, positions, and convictions without attacking those of others;

- make a clear distinction between thinking and feeling;

- accept differences between yourself and others and cope with your own anxiety about those differences;

- refuse to be defensive about your own beliefs, positions, and feelings, and refuse to demand that others justify themselves;

- maintain close contact while being open about yourself and your thoughts;
- live by whatever relationship expectations and ways of being that make sense to you, rather than living by the rules of others;
- pursue goals for yourself rather than goals for improving relationships;
- accurately "check out" what others mean and clarify with them their wants and intentions;
- negotiate, when appropriate, resolutions to differences that take into account your goals as well as the concerns of others;
- maintain a sense of self when close to significant others and self-sufficiency when distant from them;
- openly accept responsibility, undefensively, for mistakes you have made;
- use feelings to clearly and effectively express yourself;
- appreciate and enjoy the differences between you and others;
- refuse to see any family member as either saint or sinner, all good or all bad;
- don't allow yourself to be threatened or bullied or otherwise manipulated into taking responsibility for others, or do the same to others to get them to be responsible for you;
- balance an appropriate mixture of humor and seriousness, and avoid sarcasm;
- have ways to cope with your own anxiety;
- do not develop physical symptoms in reaction to stress in relationships and are not manipulated by these symptoms in others;
- are not overwhelmed by helplessness but focus instead on what your options are when others are doing something you don't like;
- do not see others as the cause of your own problems, but assume responsibility for your upset, distress, needs, etc.;
- do not make demands about how others should be or not be, or how they should feel, act, think, etc., in order for you to be happy;

- refuse to make coalitions with other family members no matter how helpful such a coalition may appear;

- establish open, non-secretive, one-to-one relationships with each significant family member;

- refuse to play the roles of persecutor, victim, or rescuer.

When you are able to achieve all this within your family of origin, you may consider yourself differentiated. And you will be the only one in the world who is! But these are the goals to work toward.

As you do change and reposition yourself in the family, the emotional mobile will become unbalanced, and others may feel disoriented and quite anxious about your changes. There is usually a three-part reaction from one or more family members. The first message is usually something along the lines of, "You are wrong, bad, selfish, irresponsible," etc. Then, "If you change back to the way you were, we will accept you again." And finally, "If you don't change, here are the terrible, punitive consequences we will mete out."

They will see your "I" position as an attack or as criticism of them. They will try to triangle in other family members or outside authorities (like a "knowledgeable" friend, a book, a doctor, a therapist, God, or a pastor or priest) to convince you that you are wrong.

The consequences that are threatened can sometimes be as extreme as violence, cutting off money or writing you out of the will, never talking to or seeing you again, withdrawing emotional investment in you (i.e., "I don't need you anymore"), getting physically ill, refusing to be happy, or being depressed and miserable "for the rest of my life because you don't love me." All kinds of things will be attempted to get you to change back. You should anticipate the kind of reaction you will get and the kind of threats that will likely be make. The less surprise there is for you the better you will be able to handle it.

It is essential that you don't give in if your effort to change is going to work. It is equally destructive if you become defensive and start justifying your actions, or in some other way become reactive.

Your basic message should be, "I understand this is upsetting to you and you don't like it, but this is the way I am going to be. This is what makes sense to me." Reactiveness on your part, including running away, will just prolong the attacks. You need to take your position and maintain closeness and openness while hearing the reaction of others in a cool, unemotional way.

Example

Cynthia had been dependently over-functioning for her 20-year-old son, fighting his battles with his dad for him and bailing him out of tough situations. She decided to stop doing this. She knew the son would be angry, which she feared, and would use the threat of cutoff. Sure enough, during the conversation when she refused to help him, he yelled and screamed at her. She remained calm, understanding, did not run away (which was her tendency in the past), and firm in her position. He left saying he was never going to see her or talk to her again and as far as he was concerned she was no longer his mother. She did not waver. Three days later he called and talked to her in a new way, with much more respect.

If you are able to maintain this stance (and you won't always), eventually the family will adapt to this change. They will reposition themselves. Frequently there is later a degree of relief and thankfulness. You may hear family members say in effect "I wouldn't have had the guts to do that" or "I'm glad you did that. I didn't really like it the way it was before. Only, don't cause any more problems like that in the future, okay?"

As stated several times, one of the goals of this work is to be able to establish a one-to-one relationship with each family member. This does not mean you have to become friends with everyone. It does mean being able to talk with any family member about any topic and maintain closeness to them even if they respond negatively to your position.

In doing this, it is essential that you neither initiate coalitions and triangles nor allow them to develop. Even talking with another family member about your ideas on changing means the two of you will share a secret, which creates a coalition. For instance, one family member may catch on to some of what you're doing and want to support you or talk to you about it and "get a few tips." Say that you're doing this for yourself and it would not be a help to you to talk about it right now.

This includes not accepting secrets either. Families are full of secrets: information that only a few people have knowledge of. And these secrets have a tremendous impact on a system. The man described earlier, whose father had a secret about a homosexual brother, is a good example of this. All along, as a boy, he had thought his father's reaction was to him, never realizing that dad was reacting to his own brother. This is what secrets do in families. They leave voids or empty places and people inevitably fill that void with their own personal fantasy about what is going on. And those who know the secret and have decided to honor it then have their hands tied. They can't react as they normally would. Important areas of discussion are ignored and avoided, or aggressively cut off. The one who knows the secret is powerless to do anything. This dynamic becomes especially difficult when a child becomes the confidant of a parent; it greatly affects the child's relation to the other parent.

We keep secrets because we think we are helping to protect someone. In fact, the secret keeps people from growing and often causes a great deal of pain as well. Whenever you agree to keep a secret, you help the family stay stuck, and as long as the secret exists, things will not change.

An excellent way to shake things up and develop the potential for change is to share openly what someone has told you in confidence. This is especially true where one person tells you about his or her feelings about another person in the family and says, "Don't tell him I said this, but ..." If you then go to the other person and say, in an unemotional way, "You know what she told me about you ... " and "I wonder why she told me rather than you?", you will provoke something! This is a good test of how non-relationship oriented you are.

One thing that may happen is that it could reduce the amount of triangling that goes on in the family. In the short run, the person who told you the secret will be angry with you for telling; but in the long run, some things may get straightened out with the other person, and they both could end up feeling grateful. Knowing you will do this, others could decide to tell you something in strictest confidence and count on you to open it up because they are afraid to. This accounts for the times when secrets are shared with those who are known as the type who can't keep secrets.

You must maintain your freedom to share a secret or not share it. You don't necessarily start blabbing all the secrets you know. Your decision to tell or not has to be based on your own effort at change and how helpful telling or not will be to that effort. Just be aware that if you are not telling because of your own uneasiness or out of loyalty or a desire to protect someone's feelings, you are making an emotional decision as a part of an unhealthy system, and you will hinder your own efforts at becoming differentiated from that system.

The use of secrets can be helpful in establishing one-to-one relationships that are difficult to get going.

Example

In an autobiographical account of his own family of origin work, Dr. Murray Bowen writes of his attempts to establish closer contact with a brother. Every time Bowen went to his hometown for a visit, his brother literally left town. Bowen tried many ways of getting some time alone with his brother, but they were all successfully avoided. Finally, he decided to make use of some family secrets. He wrote a letter to his brother in which he merely reported some of the stories other members of the family had been telling him about his brother and his brother's family. Bowen said in the letter that he wondered why family members were telling him these concerns rather than saying them directly to the brother. He sent this letter a week before his next visit. When he arrived in town, his brother was angry and eager to see him. The brother asked Bowen why he was "saying these things about me." In the process of expressing his anger, the brother unwittingly revealed a significant family triangle, which Bowen had not known about. Old misunderstandings between them were cleared up, the brother's avoidance of Bowen ended, and they developed a better relationship.

STEP 7 — REDOING IT

Do not be surprised when you do run into problems and setbacks. This work is not easy; if you're not a patient person already, you will learn to be while doing this work. Use the defeats as opportunities to learn. What did you miss? What had you not taken into account well enough? What was lacking in your hypotheses? How, specifically, do you allow yourself to be hooked?

Plan on having to go back to the drawing board to reformulate your hypotheses about what is going on and how you can be different in a way that is true to you. Map out specific strategies for dealing with the problems you encountered in the last attempt. Develop some new tactics that will not be a repeat of the last attempt since the family is "on" to that approach. Be as clear as possible about what kinds of reactions will occur and rethink how you will deal with that.

Just keep working at clarifying your own position without focusing on the rights or wrongs of others. The goal is still to be your own person — being and acting in ways that make sense and feel good to you — while being able to relate freely and warmly to others.

Doing family of origin work is neither easy nor quick. It requires patience and commitment. The man who first developed these concepts did so in the context of his own family of origin, and it took him 12 years. You have the advantage of not having to develop the concepts along the way, and can learn from the experience of others, so you shouldn't need that much time.

Be patient. Expect to make mistakes and attempt to see those mistakes as opportunities for learning rather than as failures. It took a long time to become the way you are; you will not change overnight.

But remember, there is really nothing new here. People have been doing this kind of work in their families for as long as families have existed. Those who have become mature adults, able to be themselves, have gone through a similar process. They have worked at untangling the roots, identifying who they really are, and deciding what they are responsible for. They have learned to be more accepting of themselves and others in spite of their differences.

We are all capable of doing this; I wish you success in your own journey.

Chapter
9

THE AUTHOR'S OWN FAMILY
OF ORIGIN WORK

In this concluding chapter I show how doing family of origin work has developed in my own life.

I was in my late thirties before I decided that I had to do it. I'd had about ten years of psychotherapy, off and on, before deciding this. The therapy had not led to any great changes in my life or in my relationship with wife Lois, and I felt a need to do something different. In addition, I was not happy with the kind of therapy I was providing to my clients.

Shortly after we moved from the United States to Vancouver, British Columbia, in western Canada (in 1977), I discovered Murray Bowen's *Family Systems Theory and Therapy*. This book is based on Dr. Bowen's approach. Bowen's theory became my exclusive approach to doing therapy with clients as well as my own route to personal and relationship change. Family of origin work is just one aspect of the therapy.

Bowen theory impressed me in several ways. First, it is highly respectful of people and the life difficulties they have had personally, in their marriages, and in their families. It does not divide family members into good and bad people or refer to them with words like "toxic." I hope this has been evident in this book. Not only has this been important in my own life, it has been a useful insight for my clients to develop. Secondly, it is a comprehensive approach to human relationships, seeing them in the context of the larger circumstances of their lives and especially within the emotional systems of which they are a part. Putting the self into the context of the larger emotional system within which we developed and learned to function in relationships leads not only to new understandings but also provides new ways of changing self in those relationships. This should also be evident in this book. Thirdly, Bowen theory impressed me with its inclusiveness; it was about me the therapist as well as people called "clients." It was clear that I was not any different from my clients and that we all shared the same essential humanity and similar kinds of struggles. It showed me a way to change that made sense without a lot of psychobabble.

In all the therapy I personally had over the previous years, I had talked about various family members (especially my mother) and, in general, I saw them as inadequate people who had not done enough for me or helped me to be a healthier person. Mostly, I saw their faults and they, I thought, explained my own. My therapists bought into the picture of family I presented to them and none of them suggested that I might sit down with various family members, talk with them, get to know them, or learn to see myself within the context of their lives and the emotional system of which we were all a part. I presume that my therapists were just as phobic of and judgmental of their families as I was. As a result, during those years, I never got to know any family member better and did not change the way I related to them.

When I encountered Bowen family systems theory I began a lifelong quest to understand the theory and to find ways to apply it in my own life. In addition to the changes in my family life, I began, eventually, to write about the theory. This little book is one of the first fruits of that effort, but there have been a number of other books since that show how the theory applies to different aspects of life.

1. MY OWN FAMILY CIRCUMSTANCES

I was an only child of a single mother. We lived in Columbia, Missouri for the first eleven years of my life, and then we moved to Hollywood, California where I lived, with my mother, until I finished university at UCLA. Mother was the youngest of three children. She had a sister six years older than her, and a brother three years older than her. Her mother (my biological grandmother) died just three months after my mother was born and for the first three years of mother's life the three children lived with their grandparents (my great grandparents) because my grandfather did not think he could raise them on his own. They moved back with him when he remarried about three years after the death of his first wife. Mother had a lot of the youngest sister qualities that we describe in Chapter 7 on birth order. I fit many of the characteristics that describe only male children.

From the time I was about three until age nine, we lived off and on with my grandparents; my mother's father and his second wife, mom's stepmother. Grandfather was not the doting grandparent who wanted to do a lot with his grandson. For example, as a young man, he had been a baseball player but I remember playing catch with him only once. We did practically nothing together. My grandmother was somewhat more attentive, but not hugely involved with me. She died while we were living with them and I watched her slow death for several weeks as her bed had been moved into our dining room. I was about eight years old at the time.

My mother was married four times over the years. She left my father eight months after I was born because of his infidelity. I never knew him. Immediately after leaving him, she went to work at the University of Missouri in the Vice President's typing pool. This began a lifelong career as an Executive Secretary. The second marriage happened when I was two and it lasted for only six months. When we talked about this marriage much later, while I was doing this work, mother said she had been worried about money and he had a financially secure life, but she did not love him. She left him because she realized she could not marry for money. The third marriage happened in Los Angeles when I was starting high school. It also lasted for only six months and mother also left him. The fourth marriage happened after I had finished university and was living in the eastern United States. It lasted until that husband died (for around 20 years). There were many problems with the marriage and there was one brief separation. In between each of the marriages there were several boyfriends. In each of her divorces, she never asked for alimony and she never asked my father for child support.

My mother was an independent woman who only wanted to have a sense of being loved by her husband. When each husband did not fulfil this desire, she left him and got on with her life. She did not either dependently cling to them or try to change them so that she could feel more secure. As I got to know her better, I developed a great respect for her around this. However, as she would point out, she did not always make great choices in men. All four of the men she married had significant problems with the abuse of alcohol. She never left them for this reason. She also was a liberal drinker but not to the extent of ever causing problems in her life or her work. She was a responsible worker and parent, although some modern parents might question this last part. Why I say this will become evident.

I was lucky growing up because the situation I was in, only child with a usually single parent, is a powerful relationship. If mother had tried to focus on me, and get her good feelings of being loved from me, I would have been more messed up than I was. Happily, she was not a child-focused parent. Her focus on finding a husband who would love her left me free to develop my own life without that more powerfully fused issue of me existing to make mother feel better. We had enough fusion in our life together without that issue making it more complicated. In this chapter, I will focus primarily on my family work with my mother.

1.1 My family diagram

Using the family diagram symbols I have described in this book (see Chapter 8), here is a simple presentation of my own family of origin.

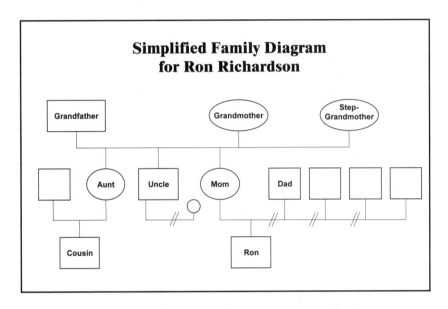

Simplified Family Diagram for Ron Richardson

The way my mother and I handled our relationship was with a lot of emotional distance. She asked very little of me and I asked little of her. She literally did not ask me many questions. When she came home each day after work we did not sit and talk about what school was like, what I had done after school, who I played with, or what my homework was, or how things were going in my life. There was none of that. Nor did she tell me about her day and I did not ask. That felt fine with me at the time. When I visited my friends in their homes, they seemed to get an unending number of questions from their parents and I was sure I would not have been happy with that. Mom relied on me not to get in trouble and to use my head.

Mother taught me about responsibility. Whenever I did something dumb or wrong she would work with me to correct it. For example, once I accidentally dropped a brick on a little girl's foot when we were playing. I ran away as she shrieked in pain. When mother got home from work and heard about the incident from the little girl's mother, mom marched me directly over to her house and made me apologize. Another time, when I was a bit older and at my own initiative, I took on a paper route that was too much for me. Frustrated, I dumped all of the papers and did not deliver them, not thinking of the consequences. Later that evening, when what I had done became clear from many phone calls from my boss, mother (in a winter snowstorm) borrowed a friend's car and we went and got the papers and delivered them. I did not keep that job but I learned that I had to follow through on what I had agreed to do.

In general, her reliance on me to do right was well founded simply because I was free to think about what was good for me. I did not have to rebel against or struggle with her. We never had a single openly angry argument. If I did get upset about something she would not let me do, I got a little pouty and she would say, "Go to your room until you can come out smiling." And that would be the end of it. Whatever the topic, it would never be raised again. We never talked anything out.

She and I never talked about my career or even schooling beyond high school. As long as I passed, grades were not an issue for her. Going to university and graduate school were all decisions I made, for myself, without consultation with her. She had never focused on my academic development or even once hinted what she thought I should do with my life. She saw that as totally my decision. She had assumed that I would get some kind of job after high school and was quite surprised that I wanted to continue with my schooling.

This way of relating to each other lasted right into my middle adult years and did not change until I began to do my family of origin work. Part of the impetus for doing this work was my marriage to Lois. Since the only lasting close relationship I had had with a woman was that with my mother, I tried to run my relationship with Lois in much the same way it had worked with my mother. It quickly became obvious that was not going to work and Lois let me know that my expectations were not normal. However, I did not have any other models to draw on. As a young person, I never really saw a husband and wife run a relationship. I do not remember even my grandparents having much of a relationship. I learned later that theirs was a hostile relationship that they managed with lots of distance. Much of my early therapy focused on how to be different in my marriage but I never really got it until I started doing my family work.

The emotional distance between mother and me was not a hostile distance; we were just apparently uninvolved in each other's lives. I always knew that she loved me but, since she rarely asked questions, I assumed she was not that interested in me and I did not express that much interest in her. As an adult, since we lived on two different coasts of the United States, I sent the regular Christmas and birthday cards, and we had a couple of phone calls a year. However, a couple of times over the years I attended conferences in Los Angeles and did not even let her know I was in town.

2. STARTING THE WORK

In doing my family of origin work, I followed the steps that I have outlined in the previous chapter. In addition, the reader can refer to Appendix I in this book where I outline a similar strategy and give specific questions that could be asked of family members. One of the first things I did was to send a copy of the family diagram (as I understood the family at that time) to each family member. In the enclosed letter, I said that I was trying to get to know my family better and asked if they would help me do this. I explained the symbols in the diagram and then asked them to tell me if anyone was missing on the diagram. I asked them to fill in missing names, dates of birth, marriage and/or divorce, and deaths. Then I asked if they could tell me anything about each person on the diagram, what they did for work, or how they spent their days, and how their life went. I thanked them again for helping me. There was no tone in the letter that I was "trying to get the dirt" on family members. I tried to communicate that I was proud of who we were and was trying to get to know "us" better.

I began doing this work with great trepidation. In reading this book, you have seen how much I emphasize asking questions. This is something my mother (and my family in general) and I did not do. I felt I was breaking a major relationship rule between us by showing interest in her life. This was new behavior on my part and it was difficult and awkward for us both at the start. One time, early in the work, I scheduled a trip to a conference in LA with the expressed intent of also spending an extra day with her. I told her that I had some questions I wanted to ask. I picked her up around 9:00 in the morning and suggested we drive down to Laguna Beach. She agreed. We spent much of the day driving around and seeing various sights, talking in very general terms. As we headed back to her house in the afternoon she said, "I thought you had some questions you wanted to ask me." I had already asked a few questions via regular mail (about the family diagram information she had provided) but this would have been our first session of sitting down face to face and talking about my questions. I was very nervous about doing it and had been avoiding it. I said, "Oh yes, how about we pull into this place for some coffee?" With about an hour left in our time together, mother and I sat and had our first ever adult-to-adult, face-to-face discussion about her growing up and her life. It was an exciting first step and she was quite open with me. The "Ned" example, also in Chapter 8, is about this event.

One of the first topics I covered with her in writing was what happened between her and my father. I had literally never asked a single question about my father and she had never volunteered any information. The "Noah" example in Chapter 8 describes what I had done with this lack of information. I created a story in my head that I must have been born out of wedlock and this is why mother never wanted to talk about him. When I sent the letter off to her asking her to tell me about my father and what happened between them, I thought I would hear an atom bomb go off down in LA. I fully expected to get a phone call along the lines of, "How dare you ask such a question?"

Instead, what I got from her were three typed pages, single-spaced, giving me the story. It was not what I had thought, as the "Noah" story details. Mom had been waiting all those years for me to ask. She had a personal rule that said, "If he wants to know he will ask." She did not know that I had a personal rule that said, "If she wants me to know, she will tell me." We had operated all of our lives with each other with these two rules in place, with neither one of us asking or telling much of anything.

I spent the first two years of my work just asking questions and being curious about her life and experiences, both in her family and on her own. I did this with other family members as well. She reported later on that her sister, my aunt, had said to her, "Ron sure is asking a lot of questions." She only replied, "He sure is." That was the end of their discussion. It was hard for me to do this simple work (at least it would be simple for many other people) but I stuck with it and she responded to my efforts. Gradually, over time, family members became more comfortable with the questions and I became more comfortable asking them. The answers were interesting, but what was more important was the fact that we were doing it and that we were developing a new kind of relationship of greater openness. During this period, my openness consisted in showing them the kinds of things I was interested in through my questions. After a while, they also began asking questions of each other, becoming curious about things they did not know about each other's lives. My mother and her sister began to develop a new, more open, and closer relationship that lasted right up until my mother's death.

It never became totally comfortable for us to talk this way and we both had to push against our hesitance. However, it is clear it became safer for us both. At one point in the later years of the work, on a visit to Vancouver, my mother agreed to make a video tape with me that I would show to my family therapy students as an example of speaking with a parent and asking questions. I was amazed that she agreed to do this. In preparation for this event, I sent her about 30 questions I might ask her in the taped interview. At the start of the taping, I said, "So I have given you the questions I might ask you today. How did they strike you?" She said, "They're nosey." I said, "Is it okay for me to be this nosey?" and she said, "We'll see."

In fact, she was open and responsive to my questions that included some personal ones like, "How do you account for your four marriages?" Her answer to that one was along the lines of, "I was looking for the love that I never felt from my father." At one point during the taped interview, she began to cry. Naturally, I feared she was upset with me, and my questions. However, I calmly asked what was going on and she said, "I so wish I could have done this with my father." I heard this as a huge affirmation of what we were doing and that she greatly appreciated the opportunity to be better known by me and to tell me her life story. I loved it as well. I learned later, after her death, that she was proud of what we were doing and had told her friends about it.

3. THE WORK PROGRESSES

I spent the first two years of my family work just asking questions about them, their lives, and their relationships with other family members. Intentionally, I did not ask any questions, or make any comments about our relationship with each other. Any questions that would have implied in some way, "Why didn't you love me more?" would have scuttled the whole effort. The other person would have become defensive and the relationship would have become antagonistic. Even if I had not intended that sort of message, the question about our relationship could be taken in a negative way. I did not want that to happen. We were doing something different with each other and that was enough up to that point. In part, I was not ready to do anything more but also I did not want to raise the anxiety too much by focusing on our relationship. In those two years, we developed a new level of comfort between us and this laid the groundwork for a safer, respectful, person-to-person, open relationship with each other.

One of the goals of this work is to develop a one-on-one relationship with every family member. This is a goal and not a starting point. Too many people rush right into family work with self-centered questions related to themselves and other family members. Very often they get a defensive response and the discussion stops or an argument develops. When people feel safer in relationships, they will gradually become more open and more vulnerable with each other. The sense of safety has to be the primary focus. Parents, for example, are very sensitive to any possible hint of accusation from an adult child of theirs that their parenting may not have been adequate. When the sense of safety is there then topics that are more sensitive can be discussed. A one-to-one relationship is achieved when two people can talk about anything in their relationship with openness and be able to hear each other with a low level of defensiveness. This does not mean they have to agree, but their disagreement does not become an occasion for hostility or greater distance between them. This level of discussion happens only as the level of safety goes up and the level of anxiety goes down.

After two years, I took a new step toward a more mutually open relationship with family members. I started letting mom know more about me, and focusing more on our relationship. At one critical point, I said to her, "You know mom, I always knew that you loved me, but I never thought you were interested in me." This is the first time I had ever focused so clearly on us and told her something about my take on our relationship over the years. If I had started the work with this kind of comment I think mother would have broken into tears, felt judged and condemned as a parent, and I would have backed off, feeling guilty for upsetting her. Moreover, that would have been the end of the discussion.

However, there was now a much higher level of safety between us and she did not have a sense that I was after her or attacking her as an inadequate or unloving parent. She was a bit shocked but also curious and said, "I have always been interested in you. Why would you think I wasn't?" I said, "Because you never, anytime, asked me any questions about my life?" She sort of slapped her hand against her forehead and said, "Oh, let me tell you what that is about." She then proceeded to tell me about her relationship with her stepmother. Mother's two older siblings had remembered, to some extent, their biological mother and had never accepted their stepmother as a parent. Theirs was a hostile and distant relationship. But my mother had been more involved with her stepmother. They were more like mother and daughter.

Mom experienced her mother as quite possessive and intrusive in her life. All through her growing up her stepmother peppered her with questions like "Where were you? Who were you with? What did you do then?" Mom said she really resented these questions and she said to herself, "When I have children, I will never do this to them." And she did not. It never occurred to her that her resolution to be non-intrusive in her son's life could have a similar negative impact just as her mother's intrusive questions did on her. She thought she was being respectful of my individuality.

This information, of course, totally reframed my understanding of mom's lack of questions. Many years of therapy had been wasted on this very basic misunderstanding. Rather than seeing it as a lack of caring on her part, I got how difficult it must have been to be interested in her son's life but feel like she did not want to pry and be intrusive like her mother had been. This struck me as an even greater expression of love and something shifted in me almost immediately around my feelings for her.

It was difficult for mother to change this stance that she had held to so firmly throughout her life. Even years later, on her deathbed, when I visited her, she said, "I know I am supposed to ask you questions about yourself, but I just can't." I said, "That is just fine mom. Now that I know you are interested, I have started telling you about anything I want you to know, rather than waiting for you to ask." This worked out just fine.

My cousin Tom, also an only child, had a much different experience growing up. His mother (my aunt) was the oldest child and her way of parenting was significantly different from how my mother (a youngest) did it. She was very child-focused. His mother was also strict and protective, keeping him close to home and always pursuing him with questions that felt intrusive to him.

Once, during the later stages of this work, my mother and I arrived in St. Louis from our different corners of the world for a family get-together. Tom picked us up at the airport and as we drove to the family home, he pointed out a building where he said he was "first allowed to stay out past midnight." I knew this must have been an issue and asked him, "How old were you then?" He said he was 19. Amazed, I turned to mother in the back seat and said, "You know, I don't ever remember us even having a discussion about what time I should get in at night." Mom said, "That's right. Because you were always in before me." This was literally true. I was never told to be in by a certain time, at any age. Hearing this, Tom made a "Harrumph" kind of sound and later told me that he had always envied the more liberal parenting I had with my mom. He had been a rebellious teenager, struggling with his more authoritarian parents, and he was often in various kinds of difficulty at school and in the community. Being more focused on not letting his parents (or other authorities) control his life, he had not spent much time thinking about or planning the kind of life he wanted for himself. He died in his late forties from complications of alcohol abuse and he had never really launched himself in life. He was living at home when he died and he had never married even though he had been a great "ladies' man." My respect for my mother's way of parenting has only grown over the years.

Mother and I began to be able to be more open with each other and I was able to say things to her that I did not think we would ever talk about. I was even able to be a resource and help to her in a number of ways. At one point, when she decided to separate from her fourth husband, I flew down to LA, helped her move out, and talked with her about what was going on. I was able to do this without getting in trouble around the triangle of her husband, her, and me. Any time she wanted to talk about him, I just responded with questions about her and made an occasional suggestion without really pushing that. Eventually (after about five months) she found a way to reunite with him which I think was good for both of them.

4. DEALING WITH TRIANGLES

One cannot do family of origin work without addressing and repositioning one's self in the family triangles. A major one for me, all through my growing up, was mom and the men in her life. With the exception of one man that I liked, I did not relate to most of the men she dated or the two men she married when I was older. To her credit she did not try to change this, but it probably made life more difficult for her.

I was trying to change my relationship with her fourth husband (the one she separated from briefly) when he died. It was difficult partly because of my attitude toward him. This attitude fed our arguments with one another over our political differences. We could have had much better discussions if my attitude had been better, but I tended to reject him and this got us nowhere. I believe I could have achieved a one-on-one relationship with him if we had had more time.

One difficulty I had with the two of them was their constant bickering and arguing, and them trying to drag me into their arguments. As a result I would distance from them both and this was part of the reason I did not like visiting them. Eventually I learned how to be present during these times and to treat it in a light kind of way, demonstrating this through various comments during their arguments, without being critical or sarcastic. When mom would complain privately to me about him I would stay away from talking about him and simply ask her questions about how she dealt with him, or what she said or did, whenever he did the negative things she described. It would have been easy for the two of us to sit and talk about how awful he was. Instead, I was simply interested in her rather than in entering into a discussion about him and whether she was right or wrong in her opinion of him. My questions seemed to help her think about her own part in their interactive process and, over time, I saw her behave differently with him and get into fewer fights with him. She was able to make use of my questions to think more about how she wanted to be with him rather than how she wanted him to be with her. She was also enjoying her life more. This was a rather successful effort at differentiating a self and being less triangled in that relationship. In addition, without my trying to make it happen or suggesting it, she better differentiated herself with her husband.

Another set of triangles emerged after he died. There were some complicated issues around him and his adult children from a previous marriage. He died being quite angry with them because of their criticisms of his drinking. Before he died, he wanted to shut them out of his will and I was able to counsel mother to not do that. I said that agreeing to his wish would be thinking with his head rather than her own. I reminded her that there were will issues in her own family history (around her stepmother's death and the fact that nothing was left to her father), and that to cooperate with her husband on this would be continuing that issue through the generations. She was in agreement with this and told her husband that his will should remain as it was, and it did. Then, after he died, she was not going to let his adult children go through his things (again thinking with his head rather than her own) and take what they wanted. I again suggested that it was only natural for them to want to do this and, as long as they were things that she did not want, she should let them do this. She did.

I tell these stories just to show that mother and I had arrived at a more open one-to-one relationship where we could say things directly to each other about our own thoughts and feelings without fear or uneasiness. Knowing I respected her, she considered my thoughts as she went ahead with her own life.

There was a triangle with my cousin Tom that took me a while to figure out. Gradually, I understood that even though we did not spend a lot of time with each other over the years, that I had a kind of older brother function for him. His mother, my aunt, had a great deal of love and respect for me and appeared to always hold me up as an example for Tom. I never knew this before doing this work but it explains why Tom refused to open up to me and tended to distance from me.

In one visit to St. Louis, I went out to dinner with him and his parents. When I came down from my room dressed in a coat and tie, he started laughing and making fun of how I tied my tie. Rather than react to his ridicule I saw a chance to change things between us. I said, "Tom, I never had a father to teach me how to tie a tie (I said this giving a glance to my uncle, his father, that recognized their relationship). Could you show me how to do it?" He jumped at the chance to teach something to me and did it with caring and enthusiasm. I was effusive in my thanks to him (again in front of his father). With an act as simple as that — me taking a one-down relationship to him — he began to be more open with me and responsive to my questions.

There was one triangle that I never knew existed until much later in my family work. My uncle Wallace had taken his own life and no one would say anything about it to me except to say he was depressed. When I asked what he was depressed about my mother and aunt would say, "He was just depressed." After asking about this quite a bit more and getting nowhere, I decided to stop pursuing the topic and dropped it. Years later, out of the blue, mom said to me one time, "Do you still want to know why Wallace was depressed?" I said, "Sure."

Then she told me the story.

Wallace had been a cook in Columbia, Missouri at a time when the racial divisions were quite strong. There was another cook in the restaurant who was black. This cook started having an affair with Wallace's wife. When "the town fathers" found out about this they marched into the kitchen one day and said to him, "Get your black ass out of town right now, or else." The cook left town immediately and Wallace's wife went with him. He sunk into a deep sense of shame about this and never recovered. After many years, he committed suicide.

This was a powerful story, of course, but then I had to wonder what had kept mom from telling it to me before. Then I got it. For the first ten years of my professional life, I had worked in the black inner-city. I was quite involved in racial issues. This was the basis of many of my arguments with her husband who had been a cop in Watts when the riots broke out there. Mom was uncertain about my reaction to her around this story because I might ask her about her reaction and what she did about it. It took her a long time to feel safe enough with me to be open about this topic. The triangle of me, her, Wallace, and racial issues had never been addressed before and we achieved a new level of openness at this point.

5. DIFFERENTIATION OF SELF

As should be clear from this brief description of my work, I did not have to struggle against my family around them keeping me from being the person I wanted to be. If my cousin Tom, for example, had attempted this work, the character of the work for him would have been quite different than it was for me.

In addition to what I have already described, my differentiation work consisted primarily in moving back toward family with interest in each family member's life and with questions. I had to find ways to connect with them, face whatever emotionality was present, and still be a non-reactive self. This felt like a huge piece of work for me and, from my perspective, it took courage. In this way, I was able to become more clearly a self with my family, and as a consequence, with other important people in my life. I was able to become present and accountable with the people I cared about.

There was one piece of differentiation I had to do in a kind of oppositional way with my mother. One reason I had not let her know in earlier years that I had come to town was that she always wanted me to spend all free time with her. When I did this nothing happened between us. She asked no questions and I volunteered no information. I wondered why I was there. I preferred to spend time with my friends. As I progressed in this work, I was able to say, "Mom, I am glad you want to see me, and I want to see you. But I also want to see my friends. When I am in LA I will be available to visit with you at these times, and at the other times I will be seeing my friends." She was not happy but she agreed to this and, because I had the sense of being there voluntarily, our visits became quite good.

Another way this work paid off in our family relationships is that I was able to be more present with them in difficult circumstances. For example, Mother contracted a rare fatal disease but showed little interest in what it was all about. Remember, she did not ask questions. I asked if I could go to her doctor with her and I showed her the questions I would like to ask him. These were questions that I wanted to know the answers to and I thought that it would be helpful for her to hear. Among other things, they included the nature of the disease, her prognosis, how long she would have to live, and specifically how death would come about. She agreed that she wanted to know the answers to these questions and asked that I go to the doctor with her. To his credit, the doctor was open and direct in his responses and did not try to avoid the discussion. This proved to be a most useful thing to do and, being a very practical woman, Mother was able to make use of the information, put all of her things in order and take care of, ahead of time, all of the usual loose ends that exist when a person dies. We were also able to talk about our lives together, to express our love, and I was present as much as possible while living over 1500 miles away. Toward the end, she agreed to let me fly her to be closer to me in northern Washington State via an air ambulance and she died not long after arriving there.

Another piece that changed for me had to do with a sense of shame that I had always carried inside me, for no clear specific reason. This sense had kept me from feeling adequate in myself. When I first presented my family to other professionals as a part of doing this work, I cried through much of the presentation because I did not think we were a good-enough family. I was ashamed of them, and, as a consequence, of myself. In doing the work my feelings about them changed. I became more and more proud of what they had managed to struggle with and to overcome. Rather than focus on their inadequacies, I saw their strengths (which I have not focused on in this brief description of the work). In a totally unanticipated way, the sense of personal shame went away as well. I have found that how people think of their family is often, deep down, how they think of themselves. My clients have also experienced this subjective shift in their own sense of self as their objective positions in their families have changed through their family of origin work.

While I think much more could have been done if my family and I could have had a longer life together, I was extremely happy that we had done so much. If I had not done this work, I am sure that I would not have been as available emotionally around all of the difficult issues that we had to deal with, and I would have been much less present and accountable. Without the work, I would have felt a tremendous sense of guilt in not letting my mother know, for example, of my love for her and my willingness to be of help. In addition, as a result of this work, I was able to be the primary resource around the death of my cousin, and then of his mother, my aunt. When they died, I was the only responsible member of my family left.

6. CONCLUSION

I regard this work as having been life changing for me personally, in my marriage to Lois, and in relation to my family and friends. In addition, I generally functioned better in the various leadership positions I have held over the years. I have seen similar changes in my clients. Some clients have had to go even more slowly with their family than I did, and many have been able to go much faster. Every client who has started the work has seen similar kinds of benefits.

I did this work without the benefit of a therapist primarily because, at the time, there was no one in Vancouver who did this kind of work. I simply studied Dr. Bowen's writing as well as I could and struggled with the questions I encountered until I could figure them out. This is, in part, why I have described this effort in this book as "self-help." In fact, I wrote this book in order to have something to give to my clients that would describe some of what was going on in families and to give them some of the tools for doing the work. This is how many other therapists and counselors have used the book.

If you, the reader, want to find professional help in doing this work, in Appendix II I have provided a list of contacts in North America that can help you find a therapist or counselor knowledgeable in doing Bowen family systems work.

$\mathcal{A}ppendix$

FAMILY RESEARCH

Here is the way Andre, who had been fairly cut off from his family, approached reconnecting with various family members. First, he drew a family diagram, or genogram (as described in Chapter 8), putting on it as many people, names, and dates as he knew. But he had many gaps on the diagram.

He sent this family diagram to all of the people who were still alive in the generations above him, on his mother's and father's sides (and including them), and to his two siblings. He included with this diagram a key to the genogram symbols.

Along with the diagram he sent the same letter to each person, the heart of which reads as follows:

"You may or may not have heard that I have become very interested in our family, and who we have been over the years. Living so far away from many of you, I have not had the opportunity to learn as much about our family as I would like. I would like to be able to tell my children someday who we are, or who we have been. Would you please help me?

"I have discovered that I don't know simple things like who is in our family. There are many names and dates of births, deaths, and marriages that I am missing. Would you please look at the enclosed diagram of our family and fill in any of the missing information that you might have or know? In some cases, I am missing actual people and you may have to add to the chart little squares or circles (see the enclosed symbol chart to know what it all means), in the order that they were born among their own sibling group. Also, if I have mixed up the order of the sibling groups that I do have, feel free to move them around to be in the correct order.

"Even if you can only add one missing name or date I would really appreciate your willingness to help. If you wish and if you request it, I would be happy to send you a copy of the finished product.

"Finally, would you please give me any information you have about these people. I'm curious about where they lived for most of their lives, their education, what work or professions they had, how their lives went generally, what interests or hobbies they pursued, their religious or faith orientation, and something about their individual personalities or characters. If they are dead, then I would like to know also of what or how they died.

"Thank you again for your willingness to help me. Family has just become so much more important to me now, and I would hate to lose any opportunity to know more about us."

He got replies from seven people of the 14 letters he sent out. They had much helpful information to share and were enthusiastic about his project. Each of them offered several anecdotes about various family members, as well the factual data he requested.

He followed up each of their replies with a thank-you letter and had a number of "clarifying questions" he asked about the information they offered. He said that rather than them having to write to him again, he might just call them "sometime soon" to chat with them about these clarifying questions.

He did this in all seven cases (three of them called him first and were very happy to talk with him — which he enjoyed also). He kept the conversations short and was simply appreciative of their willingness to share their knowledge with him. He asked just a few questions in this phone conversations about their own experience of family (like "What was it like for you being an oldest child?" or "What did you enjoy most about your family as a young person?").

Six of the seven responded well to these more personal (but still positive questions), and so he asked them if they would be willing to talk even more about their own experience of family. They all said "Sure." The seventh was suspicious and uncooperative, so Andre decided to postpone further attempts to talk to her.

Next, Andre created a list of questions somewhat like the following.

- What are some of your earliest memories?

- How did you feel "special" in your own family?

- Which parent did you feel closest to?

- What do you see as particular strengths in your family life?
- How did you and your family members deal with conflict?
- Who were you closest to in your family of origin?
- How are you different from others in your family of origin?
- How are you the same?
- What was your life like before you were married/in a relationship?
- What was your life like before I was born? At the time I was born?
- What were some of the most significant turning points in your life?
- Who are the significant people in your life?
- What goals did you establish for yourself in life? How close have you come, would you say, to accomplishing them?
- What goals do you have now?
- Who did you learn most from in your family?
- What are your most satisfying accomplishments?
- What was your biggest challenge as a partner in a marriage/relationship? As a parent?
- How did you deal with it?
- Was religion or faith important to you or your family?
- How did you develop your faith?
- What beliefs are most important to you?
- What was an important religious experience for you?
- What qualities do you appreciate most in your parents? Your siblings?
- What are some of your most important discoveries as a parent?
- How do you make decisions? Who do you talk to about them?
- How do you deal with conflict with (parents, partner, children, etc.)?
- Whose death in the family has affected you the most?

Andre also added more specific questions for each person.

He sent copies of these questions to each of the six family members (two of the family members were his own parents), along with a cassette tape, and asked them if they would be willing to tape record their answers to his questions. He said he could understand if they didn't want to do this, and maybe they could just discuss the questions someday if they ever saw each other.

All six sent him tapes full of useful and interesting information. Again, he sent letters thanking them for their help and saying how good it was to also be able to preserve the person's voice on tape.

After this process had taken place, he found it fairly easy to visit with each of these family members and begin much more personal, one-ppon-one conversations with them about family, and about their experiences as a family. He learned a great deal about the triangles and themes in the family that were previously unknown to him and which allowed him to put his own personal development in a much different perspective.

This allowed him to approach some of the difficulties and unresolved issues in his own immediate family of origin in a much more sensitive and understanding way, and he let go of some of his resentment and upsetting feelings about family experiences and about his own life generally. He began to feel, at age 42, that he was "becoming a real adult."

If you have better connections with your family members than Andre did, you may not have to move at his pace to get in touch with your family. His method is for those who need to take it slower and who may be unsure of their own willingness to get further involved with family, and those unsure of the willingness of various family members.

$\mathcal{A}ppendix$

II

FINDING PROFESSIONAL HELP
FOR DOING FAMILY OF ORIGIN WORK

While the term "self-help" is in the sub-title of this book, I actually wrote it as a guide for my clients doing counseling work with me. I wanted something I could give them that was a simple description of what this work was about and how it proceeded. Many other counselors and therapists have used this book with their clients for this same purpose. A person could use the information in this book, on their own, without benefit of professional help. It describes the kind of work more mature people have been doing within their families for centuries, long before there was such a thing as "helping professionals." However, working with a person trained in Bowen theory will help a great deal in better understanding what the work is about and how to proceed in doing it.

In searching for a counselor, the important consideration is finding one who views the family as a positive resource instead of seeing clients as unfortunate victims of toxic family members. Whether a person is called a counselor or a therapist does not matter a great deal. I use both terms interchangeably. These terms refer more to the professional associations they belong to than to the kind of work they do. Psychiatrists, psychologists, marriage and family therapists, pastoral counselors, social workers, and many other kinds of trained helping professionals can provide their clients this kind of specialized help.

Dr. Bowen, who was a psychiatrist, and who taught psychiatry at Georgetown University in Washington, DC, preferred to call himself a "coach" with his patients. This recognized that the patients were the ones out on the field of play, doing the work. The work was not so much in the relationship with the counselor but in what patients could do in relation to their family. That is how I saw my own work as a therapist, and that is the assumption that lies behind this book.

Since there is no professional association of Bowen theory therapists, and since they are represented by a variety of professional designations, they are hard to find. The reader may have to interview a number of counselors in order to find one that can help them with this approach. The kinds of questions I would ask in such an interview are:

- Do you see a person's family as a positive resource in their own emotional development?

- Do you see the individual as part of a larger emotional system and, if so, do you think about how to create change for the person in that context?

- Are you familiar with Bowen theory and with family of origin work?

- Have you had training in that approach?

- Are you doing your own family of origin work?

I provide below a partial list of training centers in Bowen theory for professionals who want to do this kind of work with clients. Even if a center is not located close to where you are, they may be able to refer you to a trained professional in your area.

The primary center for training in Bowen theory is located in Washington, DC. It is the Bowen Center for the Study of the Family (www.thebowencenter.org). The phone number is 1-800-432-6882. They are in touch with therapists all over the world as well as in North America and may be able to help in making a recommendation. Here are the locations, names, phone numbers, and websites for a number of other centers.

1. North Vancouver, British Columbia (Canada)
   Living Systems
   604-926-5496
   www.livingsystems.ca

2. Chula Vista, California
   Southern California Education and Training in Bowen Family
     Systems Theory
   619-525-7747
   www.socalbowentheory.com

3. Sebastopol, California
   Programs in Bowen Theory
   707-823-1848
   www.programsinbowentheory.org

4. Delray, Florida
   The Florida Family Research Network, Inc.
   561-279-0861
   www.ffrnbowentheory.org

5. Wilmette Illinois
   The Center for Family Consultation
   847-866-7357
   www.thecenterforfamilyconsultation.com

6. Potomac, Maryland
   The Center for Family Process
   www.centerforfamilyprocess.com

7. Dorchester, Massachusetts
   New England Seminar on Bowen Theory
   www.bowentheoryne.org

8. Kansas City, Missouri
   Kansas City Center for Family and Organizational Systems
   816-436-1721
   www.kcfamilysystems.com

9. Princeton, New Jersey
   Princeton Family Center for Education, Inc.
   609-924-0514
   www.princetonfamilycenter.org

10. Rochester, New York
    Leadership Coaching, Inc.
    585-381-9040
    www.leadershipcoachinginc.com

11. Pittsburgh, Pennsylvania
    Western Pennsylvania Family Center
    412-362-2295
    www.wpfc.net

12. Austin, Texas
    Side by Side, Inc.
    800-204-3118
    www.sidebyside.com

13. Houston, Texas
    Center for the Study of Natural Systems and the Family
    713-790-0226
    www.csnsf.org

14. Essex Junction, Vermont
    Vermont Center for Family Studies
    802-658-4800
    www.vermontcenterforfamilystudies.org

15. Washington, DC
    The Learning Space
    202-966-1145
    www.thelearningspacedc.com